The Last World Of The Caucasus

THE LOST WORLD
OF THE
CAUCASUS

The Lost World
of the
Caucasus

BY

Negley
Farson

1958
DOUBLEDAY & COMPANY, INC.
Garden City, New York

FIRST PUBLISHED IN THE UNITED STATES OF AMERICA 1958
LIBRARY OF CONGRESS CATALOG CARD NUMBER 58-6265

To the Memory of
Alexander Wicksteed

CONTENTS

ILLUSTRATIONS

RESURRECTION

NO matter that men in their hundreds of thousands disfigured the land on which they swarmed, paved the ground with stones so that no green thing could grow, filled the air with the fumes of coal and gas, lopped back all the trees and drove away every animal and every bird: spring was still spring in the town. The sun shone · warmly, the' grass came to life again and showed its green wherever it was not scraped away, between the paving stones as well as on the lawns and boulevards; the birches, the wild cherries, and the poplars unfolded their sticky and fragrant leaves, the swelling buds were bursting on the lime trees; the jackdaws, the sparrows, and the pigeons were happy and busy over their nests, and the flies, warmed by the sunshine, hummed gaily along the walls. Plants, birds, insects, and children rejoiced. But men, adult men, never ceased to cheat and harass their fellows and themselves. What men considered sacred and important was not the spring morning, not the beauty of God's world given for the enjoyment of all creatures, not the beauty which inclines the heart to peace and love and concord. What men considered sacred and important were their own devices for wielding power over their fellow men.—*Tolstoy*, 1899.

I

IN the spring of 1929 I set out to ride horseback over the Western
Caucasus with Alexander Wicksteed, an old English eccentric who,
for six years, had been trying to live like a Russian in Red Moscow.
Our intentions were to get the first pair of horses at Kislovodsk, then
to proceed by easy stages, camping out on the northern spurs of the
Caucasus wherever we liked a place, or I found some good trout
fishing; finally, to try and take our horses over the snow-clad Klukhor
Pass (9,400 feet) and ride down beside the foaming river Kodor to
the melon beds of Sukhuum on the shores of the Black Sea.

We did not think this would require any mountain work of much
consequence, or knowledge of snow faces· that education was to
come. Nor did we know that the spring is the worst of the rainy
seasons in the Western Caucasus, and that for a large part of our ride
we would be lashed by hailstorms, say up at 8,000 feet, which would
only turn into pelting rain when we sought shelter lower down.
[Interesting example of how wet we usually were: our horse-wrangler
used to *strop* the reins every morning, pulling them back and forth
across the handle of the hatchet. These reins were not exactly rawhide, but they were primitive (see those of the two horsemen,
facing page 64) ; and these Caucasian mountaineers, practically
born in the saddle, are some of the finest horsemen in the world.]
We even had snow. There were nights, making camp, when we
did not have a dry spot on us. However, when we did manage to
get cover over our heads, these things made it only the more com-
panionable. And when the Caucasus did break through their veil of
clouds, and we crawled out of our tent in the mornings to see the
snowfields of the main range being gilded by the sun, we knew that
we were having one of the most deeply satisfying experiences of
our lives.

Strange as it may seem, for they are among the wildest mountains
on earth, the one thing you feel most about the lonely places of the

· 13 ·

Caucasus is a deep personal tenderness, a brotherhood; and the aching wish, vain as you know it to be, that you could guard their rare beauty. They "possess" you. Once you have felt the spell of the Caucasus you will never get over it.

My reasons for writing this book now, some twenty years after Wicksteed and I made this ride, are: first, I have always wanted to write the full story of this trip—to sit down some day with my note-books, made on the Russian rivers and in the Caucasus, and write this journey against the background of its times; not the censored, necessarily condensed accounts that appeared in newspaper articles. A journey such as this, with all the notes that one makes, is a possession. Writers will know how one keeps such things—a story that can be told only once—until the time, or the mood, or some current events impel you to write it. These events occurred in the spring of 1950, when news began to leak to the outside world of Stalin's ruthless deportation of entire Caucasian tribes to the wastes of Siberia: the Tchetchens, the Inguish, the Balkars. This was closely followed by the news that some 750 families of the Kalmucks, who had managed to escape from the slave-pen of Soviet Russia, had been given land and the chance to make a new life in South America, in Paraguay. This dramatic finish of at least one branch of the horse-men who rode out of Asia, following the Golden Horde, can be put against the time when I saw them; nomads of the southern steppes or fishermen on the Caspian, still filled with the dreams invoked by the short-lived Kalmuck Republic. These notes that I made were literally a last look at a lost world.

We had both been in the Caucasus before. Wicksteed, who had reached Tashkent and semi-forbidden Samarkand in 1923, had made some walking trips through the Karachaite country of the Caucasus in the summers of 1926 and 1927; but this would be the first time that he had ever "penetrated" to their capital, as he liked to put it. I had been down in the Eastern Caucasus the year before; landing at Makhach-Kala, in Daghestan, from an ancient paddle-wheeler in which I had only just survived a monstrous storm in the shallow Caspian, together with a deck-load of sea-sick Persians, Turks, Tartars, Georgians, Daghestaniis, Tchetchens, etc., etc., most of them howling to Allah; and an arrogant Russian Peoples Commissar and his party who, so the captain told me, were going down to the Caucasus to shoot bear—with a machine-gun.

It was exciting. The Georgian Military Road from Vladikavkaz, the "Key to the Caucasus," over the Krestovi Pass (7,695 feet) to Tiflis, must be one of the most sensationally beautiful mountain highways in the world. In the gorges of the wild Terek you see the river smoking among its black rocks a thousand feet below, the walls of sheer rock rising thousands of feet straight over your head; and beyond, in the gap, the eternal snows of Mt. Kazbek looming under their cap of clouds. From the crests of high passes you catch glimpses of other snows on the main range, running high along the sky.

But you never get near them. You will know nothing of the real Caucasus if you stick to the main roads. There are twelve peaks in the Caucasus that are higher than Mt. Blanc (15,780 feet). And between Mt. Kazbek (16,545), which stands only seventh in line, and Mt. Elbruz (18,784) there are 125 miles of glaciers, ice, and snow. The Frosty Caucasus, the early English climbers called them. There is one place in the Central Group where, within a space of only ten square miles, there are *twenty* peaks of over 14,000 feet. There are 900 glaciers in the Caucasus, several of which are exceeded in length only by the Aletsch. The glaciers on Mt. Elbruz alone cover 83 square miles. The snowfall in the Caucasus is higher than in the Central Alps. There are only two main passes over this 125 miles of the frozen main chain: the Krestovi, and the Mamison (9,265) which is higher than the Stelvio. All the rest are merely horse-trails, bridle-paths, at an average elevation of 10,000 feet. Some tribes of the Caucasus are so snow-bound that you can get into their valleys only at certain times of the year.

The immense height and wildness of the great snowy ranges; the furious rivers, which have cut gorges thousands of feet deep; the vast spread of the primeval forests—all these have made the Caucasus a refuge for man, the outlawed and oppressed, since before recorded history. The origin of many of the present-day tribes is still unknown. This wildness of the country enabled the Caucasians to hold off the advancing Slavs, the Great Russians, for over 160 years of continuous fighting, probably the fiercest mountain warfare ever known. Moscow was not able to announce the final conquest of the Caucasus until 1864. The mountain chain itself, which separates Europe from Asia, is some 650 miles long, running east-south-east from Novorossesk on on the Black Sea to Baku on the Caspian. But the really mountainous

· 15 ·

part is about 400 miles, with skirts of 100 to 150 miles; and the 125 miles of everlasting snow between Mt. Kazbek and Mt. Elbruz contain all the main peaks. The wildness of the country also prevented the Caucasian tribes from fully co-operating with each other against the Russians: they had been accustomed to raiding and robbing each other for centuries. These mountains contain a greater number of tribes, races, and peoples than any similar extent of territory on the surface of the globe; speaking, too, a greater variety of languages. They were known and deeply feared by the ancient Greeks, who followed the olive tree wherever it would grow, around the shores of the Black Sea. It was to Mt. Elbruz that Zeus chained Prometheus after he had stolen fire from the gods and given it to man. It was these eternal snows "hanging in the sky" that Jason and his Argonauts saw from their bark in the sweltering Black Sea, which made them think they had reached the edge of the world. Beyond those silvered snows appearing far above the tumult of the clouds lay the Infinite. And it was in these same snows on the flanks of Mt. Elbruz that I was locked on the night of June 27th, 1929, which made me think I had reached the end of the world too.

Douglas W. Freshfield, Englishman, was the first man to conquer three of the most formidable Caucasian peaks. He made his first ascent of Elbruz in 1868, only four years after the Russians had conquered the Caucasians, when the remote mountains were still made dangerous by man as well as by avalanches and glaciers. On page 177, vol. II, of his splendid book *The Exploration of the Caucasus* you will see a photograph of this very glacial lake on whose edge I was frozen in. This photograph must have been taken in late July or August, when the Klukhor is comparatively free from snow. When I was there in June the shores of this lake were a foot or more deep in snow; the lake itself was still frozen over, with green patches of melting ice, and the repeated sound of snow and ice and chunks of glacier falling in it. And at its mouth, where it poured over in a steady stream to fall a thousand or so feet into the ravine I had just come up, there were two overhanging shelves of snow-covered ice which were so weak that one broke with me when I crossed the lip the next morning just after sunrise. No horse except Pegasus could have made it.

It is said that in the immense solitude of high mountains you come closer to knowing yourself than you will anywhere else on earth, not that that can always be a comfort. I had plenty of time that night to think about this. I had to send Yusef back with the two horses, after we had struggled all afternoon to get them up to this 9,000 feet. At about 7,000 feet we met snowfields. Where we were in the shade of the peaks the snow-crust was strong enough to bear them. Crossing the wide fields, turning to glistening slush in the sun, they frequently punched through and sank in up to their bellies. To get them on their feet again we had to pull them on their sides, and then right them. Sometimes we made only a few yards. Their fortitude was sublime. When we reached the bridle path that is now the Klukhor trail— the old Sukhuum Military Road had long since been broken off the cliffs in places by frost and sun—it was still a stiff climb, though otherwise easy going. I sent Yusef back with two orders: one was to tell the two G.P.U. guards we had met in the valley far below just what swine. we thought they were for telling us, so glibly, that the Klukhor was open to horses (I doubt if either of them had ever been up to this lake); the other was to find another porter, somehow, and bring him back to help carry what little I would now take of my kit over the peak of the Klukhor. Then Yusef and I would walk down to the Black Sea.

The sinking sun was just sliding down behind the cold grey peaks when Yusef left me. I tried to make some tea using the "solid heat" tablets from my medical kit; but either the altitude or the wind stopped me from ever getting the water hot enough. However, I had plenty of cigarettes, so I huddled down in the lee of some rocks that some former person had piled up against the wind that sweeps this pass, and watched night come on. It was beautiful, with the last spears of rock being gilded by the sun. Then grey darkness and a mist swept over. This cleared later on. And against a bowl of stars I watched that "weird Dru-like needle" that so impressed Freshfield, and saw, at different places along the night sky, the glint of white snow. The ledge was very narrow and I was afraid to fall asleep. I need not have worried: it was like spending the night in a refrigerator. And, to give you some idea of the faithfulness and skill of these Teberdine guides, Yusef came back in the hours of darkness, with another Mohammedan, and climbed over the edge of my shelf just before day broke. We started to cross the dome of the Klukhor, after I had fallen in the lake, while our shadows were still long with the rising sun.

To get an acute picture, like that, of what the Frosty Caucasus can be really like, although parts of it do look better in retrospect, you have to leave all roads, big or small, and strike into the mountains on horse or on foot. There were three weeks on this trip when Wicker and I never saw a road, and several days when we were not even following trails.

My first trip to the Eastern Caucasus had, by comparison, been a conventional journey. But with a strong sense of history at every turn of it:

> "Nor is this surprising" [wrote John Baddeley, another Englishman, in *The Russian Conquest of the Caucasus*, that stirring book to which he devoted his entire life], "for the whole country teemed with memories of fighting days, and wherever we rode, wherever we rested—in walled cities, in villages, on the hills or the plains, in forest depths, in mountain fastnesses—there were tales to tell of desperate deeds, of brave adventures, the battle shock of armies, the slaughter of thousands, the death of heroes. Dull, indeed, must be he whose blood is not stirred in a land so varied and beautiful, filled with memories so poignant."

This bloodthirsty pæan to the glory of military murder strikes an unpleasant note these days. But the Caucasians were great warriors. I like Freshfield's reason for why he went to the Caucasus, because it expresses the poet so ever-present in the romantic, world-wandering Englishman:

> "As an Eton boy I had reached the Sixth Form and the top of Mt. Blanc at about the same period. When, in 1868, my Oxford terms were over, and I had a larger opportunity of indulging my love of mountain travel, the sonorous phrases of *Prometheus Vinctus* were ringing freshly in my ears. . . ."

So he set out to climb Elbruz. The book he wrote twenty-eight years later is still exciting; good for many and many a night of wild winter's reading. In it he asserts that there were several lesser summits, and many other glacial expeditions, that were of greater difficulty than his three famous first-ascents: Elbruz, Kazbek, and Tetnuld. He has a brittle wit and a spicy contempt for the "scientist," the geographer "who hardly ever, if at all, penetrated above the snow level," and "whose real knowledge could be likened to the '*ascensions du Mont*

Blanc jusqu'au Montenvers.' " Freshfield was then President of the Alpine Club.

The railway going inland from Makhach-Kala runs along the foothills of Daghestan, and across part of the high mountainous plateau where the rivers have cut gorges 2,000 to 3,000 feet deep to escape from their prison of the Caucasus. This bare and beautifully barbaric land was the country of the great Shamil, the Mohammedan mystic who raised a *jehad*, a holy war, against the Russians in 1829—twenty-seven years after the Russians and the Cossacks of the line thought they had absorbed and tamed the country. For the next thirty years, the wild, mountainous plateau of Daghestan was the scene of some of the most desperately brave guerilla warfare ever known. No quarter was asked or given on either side. When the Mohammedan women of an *aoul*, a mountain village, saw that all was lost they, nearly always, threw their children over the precipices and jumped after them. The men fought until the last man was cut down. This thirty years' continuous fighting was known as the Murid war—Muridism originally being a means of spiritual perfection, a supreme development of Sufi'ism, introduced by the Arab conquerors into Daghestan in the eighth century—and the Murids fought the Russians with the fanaticism of men who had renounced all earthly things. It was a formidable display of the power of the spirit; what can be done by an idea. And this was responded to by something in the Russian spirit; for, with all their luxury, the arms-bearing Russian aristocracy were not materialists, really. They rose to deeds of valour, of comradeship, and self-sacrifice in the Caucasus that they have probably never equalled in all their courageous history. If it is true that "mountains make the man," the Caucasus provide many noble examples.

Therefore it was quite the thing for the Russian officers of that time, young bloods from Moscow, to serve a few years in the heroic Army of the Caucasus (as had Tolstoy); and it takes nothing from the glory of it that this was usually done to economise and pay their gambling debts. These officers had to lead their men up cliffs, hand over hand, to take by the sword and bayonet villages that were built on the edges of yawning ravines, like eagles' nests, defended by some of the most desperate fighters that this world has ever known. In some engagements the Russians made human ladders of themselves, climbing on each other's shoulders, while the mountaineers poured

· 19 ·

rifle fire on them and hurled down heavy beams. And in at least one fight the Russian officers actually had themselves lowered in baskets, so that they could get at the fierce tribesmen sheltering on a ledge; and there, with a desperation and savagery that were almost sublime, they fought with the Caucasians, man to man, sword to sword. It was the same on both sides. "*No braver man, no keener blade*" was carved on Hadji Mourad's sword.

Sacheverell Sitwell, in *Valse des Fleurs*, gives a picture of Shamil's son, who was captured, as a Caucasian dandy at the Winter Palace in St. Petersburg, a splendid officer of the Guards; with, from all accounts, all the pretty women at his feet, or in his bed. He was eventually ransomed by his father, exchanged for several high-ranking Russian officers, and was brought back to his eagle's nest and the bitter freedoms of the Caucasus, where, pining for the voluptuousness of the Imperial Court, he sickened and died.

Shamil (who had trained himself as an athlete: he was said to be able to jump twenty-seven feet!) travelled with his own executioner, threw his Russian officer prisoners into pits, and he kept them there like wild animals, even flayed them alive. His father had been a notorious drunkard; and to cure him Shamil said, when he was cleansing the Mohammedan spirit for the fierce Murid fighting, that the next time he saw his father drunk he would kill himself in his father's presence. It worked. His other side was that he had a cat, which always sat at the table with him, which he loved above everything else in this world, and fed with his own hands every meal, before he would allow himself or anyone else to eat. When the cat died, Shamil was plunged in gloom: he said, "This is the end of me." And so it was; he was surrounded and captured shortly after, after thirty years during which he had escaped every trap. He made one pilgrimage to Mecca, then returned to Russia and his favourite wife, a beautiful Georgian aristocrat who had followed him into captivity; and eventually died, an old white-bearded patriarch, more honoured by the Russians than even their own generals.

I went inland along the southern foothills of the Terek river, the country in which the young Tolstoy served for three years as a Russian officer with the Cossacks of the Line; from which wildly romantic experience of fighting and love he wrote that lovely little classic *The Cossacks*, the one book of his which the old Russians, even Turgenev, loved and admired most of all his books, more even

. . a shy, handsome young man, obviously the son of the Old Man of the tribe . . .

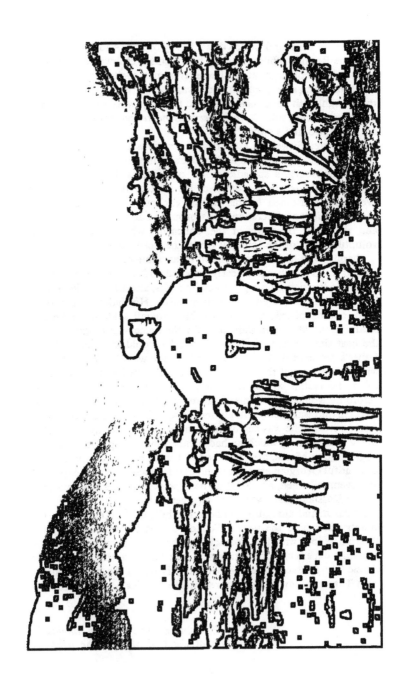

than *War and Peace*. The haunting, painfully nostalgic love story of the young Russian officer for the untamable Cossack girl—and his strange fascination and love for her Cossack lover—are Tolstoy's own story. And no one could have invented that lovable old rascal, Uncle Eroshka. That beautiful little book is full of *experienced* love, and the breath-taking romance of the wild Caucasus. Tolstoy spent his three years fighting against the Tchetchens, the Tartar race who lived in the deep beech forests across the Terek; forests so dense (some of the immense beeches were thirty-five feet in circumference) that the Tchetchens could not be conquered until the "great" Yermolov, who ordered women and children to be butchered, had corridors cut through them that were a musket-shot's width on either side of his invading columns. So that the Tchetchens, who finally had to surrender in 1864, had at least the sad consolation of being able to say that they were beaten by the axe and not the sword.

It is just as well to know these things when you travel in the Caucasus. Every trail, every cliff then has its story. You can recreate the scenes of the past. In the wild and romantic life that they lived fighting these mountaineers, the "outlaws" as Moscow had labelled them, many a Russian aristocrat, exiled from Slav society because of his too liberal views (as was Lermontov), found a kinship with these scenes and with the very men he was out to kill; refused to return to Slav Russia, and ended his days soldiering in the heroic Army of the Caucasus. And once you have felt the spell of the Caucasus you will read again and again, with a heartache to get back to these magic mountains, Lermontov's poignant book *A Hero of Our Times*. I carried *The Cossacks* with me on my return to the Caucasus as well as Gogol's *Taras Bulba*. I read them, once again, by Caucasian campfires. The ultimate end of the Tchetchens, as a Caucasian tribe, came only the other day. During the year 1945, together with the Inguish and the Balkars, probably the three finest tribes still left in the Caucasus, they were deported by Stalin to the wastes of Siberia. But they are still rebelling against Moscow: London newspaper accounts as I write this (July 1950) say that some of these deported Tchetchens have made their way back to the Caucasus from Siberia, and are again "making trouble for the Russians." I sincerely hope they are. They are in the tradition.

The Kalmucks, who came into the Northern Caucasus in the thirteenth century with Batu, the grandson of Genghis Khan, and settled as nomads on the vast steppes, were persuaded to side with the Russians and Cossacks against the wild mountain tribesmen lower south. They were part of the army of Peter the Great when, in 1722, he began his futile effort to conquer the Caucasus—part of an army, 82,000 infantry, all veterans of the Swedish war, 9,000 dragoons, and about 70,000 Cossacks, Kalmucks, and Tartars. The Kalmucks were launched against the Tchetchens, who cut them up unmercifully; the remainder of Peter's army was signally defeated by the Mohammedans of Daghestan. The effort was fiasco. (And 130 years later, Tolstoy, as a young officer, was still fighting the Tchetchens across the Terek on the same spot from which they had thrown the Kalmucks). In 1771, disgusted by the treatment they had received from their Russian allies, all the broken promises, a vast horde of Kalmucks assembled on the east bank of the Volga, struck their tents, and with their herds of cattle and flocks of sheep tried to get back to China. Less than a third of the 300,000 Kalmucks ever reached the Chinese frontier. Their return path across Asia was marked by their skeletons. The nomadic tribesmen who remained in Russia sided with the White Russians and the Kuban Cossacks in the civil war which followed the Revolution of 1917. Many of them succeeded in leaving Russia and emigrated to the Balkans. In the aftermath, when it really did look as if the U.S.S.R. was going to be a composite of free, independent nations, a Kalmuck Republic was established. Then in this last war the Kalmucks sided with the Germans when they invaded the Caucasus—sided with anyone, so long as he was against Moscow—and in 1943 the Kalmuck Republic was liquidated. The 200,000 Kalmucks who had composed it Stalin deported to Siberia. The same old story. But not quite. The last time the Kalmucks appeared in the world's news was in 1950, when it was announced that Paraguay, of all places, had given 750 Kalmuck families 9,000 acres of fine farming land, and sanctuary to live as they pleased, with their own language, their own religion. These were the Kalmucks who had fled with the retreating German forces and become "displaced persons" in Germany, most of whom the Allies found in concentration camps. The Kalmucks are Buddhists, and this is the first time that that religion has been brought to the continent of South America. The word Kalmuck, appropriately, means remnant.

In 1864, when they finally had to surrender to the Tsar's armies,

400,000 Circassians, perhaps the finest horsemen in the world, emigrated *en masse* to all parts of the world rather than accept the rule of Moscow. Their forefathers had, long since, been sold as slaves by their own nobles—for the trade in human flesh was always strong in the wild Caucasus—and had become the Janissaries of the Turkish sultans; the Mamluk Corps, for so long the real masters of Egypt; the "most fashionable" eunuchs—and the favoured Circassian slave of the Persian and Turkish harems. Most of the noble families of Persia have been bred from Circassian mothers.

On my first trip to the Caucasus, made in the late autumn of 1928, I went on to Tiflis, through mellow Georgia, and on to Baku where the oil derricks rise like a dark forest from the foreshore of the shallow Caspian. Intensely interesting; but a journey marred at every turn by the bombastic cocksureness of the young Communists, who were very hard to put up with at that time, and have become worse as they grew up. Perhaps the only two worth-while memories that I would like to keep from that trip are my meeting with the Khevsurs, up a side valley north of Tiflis, and a few days I spent with the Württemberg Germans. The Khevsurs are one of the several races of the Caucasus whose origin is still unknown. Many of them have red hair and blue eyes; they wear coats of chain mail on ceremonial occasions, and, at all times, they carry a round, bossed shield and a sword strikingly similar to those borne by the Crusaders—from whom they, and many competent historians, believe they are descended. Their homes are built in tiers up the mountainsides, reminding one of the cities of Tibet; and they have stone watch-towers in their defiles that are almost identical with those you will see up the Khyber Pass. They are the worst drunks in the Caucasus.

The Württemberg Germans lived in a beautiful little village the other side of Tiflis, rich with vines, apricots, and apple orchards. They spoke absolutely pure German, lived by German customs. They were all that was left of 1,700 families who had set out from Württemberg in 1817 to reach Mt. Ararat—to meet the Second Coming of Christ. Their Protestant ministers had worked it out that He would appear on Mt. Ararat in 1834. They reached Odessa, where only one hundred families survived the plague; and Alexander I gave them land in the Caucasus, where they established this prosperous little community of Marienfeld. But they are there no more. Stalin moved them all to the wastes of Siberia during the last war.

That was the Eastern Caucasus, about which I shall write no more in this book. In fact, I would be ashamed to. that part of Russia has now become so much a standard part of the "Soviet Route," down which it funnels visiting British M.P.s, Trade Union delegates, and prominent British playwrights, whom it wishes to impress, and, in turn, have them return to their own countries to impress the outside world with the paradise of life under the Soviets, that it is almost loathsome to think about. The whole thing from the Polish frontier to Baku on the Caspian is a Soviet set-up. This book is about the Western Caucasus. I cite the Khevsurs and the Württemberg Germans merely as two odd bits in the human mosaic of the Caucasus, in whose pockets the tides of history have left seeds of almost every race, even of the Norsemen who ventured down the Dnieper after founding Kiev. These wild mountains, as I have said, have always been a refuge for the outlawed and oppressed, or the bold and more fanatically freedom-loving people. And the higher and smaller the pocket of people the more sharply, it seemed, did they cling to their own distinctions of race and tongue. The very trails by which Wicksteed and I hoped to cross the Main Range led to a country on the shores of the Black Sea where some twenty distinct languages, or dialects that have become almost different languages, can be heard today; the country in which Pliny says the Romans conducted their affairs through 134 interpreters.

Al-Aziz called the Caucasus "The Mountain of Tongues." Once Wicksteed and I had left Kislovodsk, and crossed over the first mountain range, we found that our own knowledge of Russian was no longer of any use to us. In the country of the Turko-Tartars we began to converse in sign language.

Old Wicksteed was going to walk the whole of this journey through the Western Caucasus. There were times when I could have murdered him for his obstinacy, and times when he made me almost weep. To be forced to look down, on some particularly wretched sunset, and see that old man squelching along, staff in hand, water shooting from his grey beard as from any gargoyle—and *proud* of his absolute wretchedness! He would not change places with me on the horse: nothing could make him. I was embarrassed by my own shelter against the weather, the heavy Caucasian *burka*, that broad-shouldered felt cloak that no rain can penetrate; yet so immensely heavy that old Wicker could not have carried it more than a mile or so on foot. I even rode in heavy rain without my *burka*, just to shame him; not to let him get entirely away with his triumph that, even though he did happen to be many years my senior, he was just as good as I was, if not better. It was impossible to humiliate him. But we had some nights and days that I shall never forget; although a few were so beautiful and delicate in their poetry that I could not even put them down in my notebook at the time. These are the scenes, with the emotions they evoke in you, which you must leave to the perspective of time: one day—take their residue. These are the things from travel that you hardly ever sell. But they are yours; and they are almost invariably travel's greatest rewards.

I came out of a deep pine forest on to a lip of the Caucasus one sunset, and there, sitting on my horse, I watched for as far as my eyes could see some fifty, sixty, possibly a hundred miles of snows change colours in the sunset. I watched them run the sequence of colour in the dying rays. This was the unbelievable sight, after wandering for weeks up the valleys of the lower ranges, where the mountains rose all around us, shutting us off from the sky, suddenly to see the great Main Range again. There it lay, that immense 400-mile range of mountains that throughout history has separated Europe from Asia. Stretching away in rocks, cliffs, pinnacles, gleaming snowfields; the 125 miles of snow and ice between Mts. Kazbek and Elbruz. I could almost hear that "silence between the spaces" as I watched the unbroken snows of the main chain take on their rosy glow, change from rose to violet, then a deep gentian, until every detail below me began to merge in utter darkness. Then the last rays of the sun tipped the ridge of the main range with brilliant gold. A thread of gold so improbable, fading like a drift of smoke, that I wondered if it had been there at all. Directly below me, while the light lasted, I had looked down at the tops of a pine forest, so far below that its jagged tips looked like a smooth bluish plain. And where it ran white with its rapids I could pick out the river up whose valley we had been riding the last few days.

For the last few days Wicksteed and I had been riding with a tribe of Tartars who were taking their animals, their sheep and their goats, their cattle and their horses, over the lower ranges of the Caucasus in search of grass. It was a yearly migration, which the same tribe had probably been making for centuries, and over the same trails. The roots of the trees in the forests we had come through were so rubbed bare by the hoofs of animals that in some of the darker stretches they lay ahead of us like a road of white bones. Forests of beech, of oak, and of tamarisk. Dark scented pines. In the clearings of some of the beech forests our horses waded belly-deep through azalias and tiger-lilies. In some the dense fountain-like ferns were over our horses' heads. Then there were immense, maddening stretches of flowering rhododendrons; beautiful to look at, but abso-lute hell to have to take cattle through. The youngest children were tied to the saddles, their heads wobbling wildly, and they added their cries to the bawling and bleating of the animals. The old folks rode silently, dejected, because for some this would undoubtedly be the last journey; and they all had to hang on grimly as in the steep ascents our little Caucasian horses scratched and scrambled, clawing their way up like cats. In the nights, when we made camp, you could hear half a hundred udders being milked.

I had ridden on ahead, leaving Wicksteed and the Tartars to come on. I wanted solitude, the scene all to myself. This lip in the Caucasus was like a shelf along the edge of a world in which men lived a life that was almost completely cut off from it. Riding along the precipice now, I looked down to my left and saw that I was looking down into the great green bowl. There was a small lake at the bottom of it, just a mountain tarn, for there are few lakes in the Caucasus. And there I saw running free, or still placidly grazing, horses and their foals. And a cluster of cabins made from uncut logs. I waited for the Tartar cavalcade to come up with me. For, shut up as they have been for centuries among the pockets of the Caucasus, each tribe has developed—or maintained—its own distinct code of what it thinks are the best manners. And etiquette must be obeyed.

Looking down, I saw that this tribe had made a prodigal use of its background—the dark wall of pine forest. I saw that the goats and the sheep and the cows were being herded for the night into immense corrals made from entire tree trunks. Flocks of bleating kids were being hurried up from their grazing bowl by boy shepherds. The great grey bulls and bullocks were being allowed to stay out in the open, to roam through the dew that would soon turn this green bowl into silver in the moonlight. (The weaker animals were being corralled because of wolves. This remote pocket of people, just on the edge of the timber line, was one of the two that Wicker and I stayed with in the Caucasus where they had the "wolf-fires" going all night. Big fires at the four quarters of the settlement, with boys pushing the big logs into the fire as they burned. It was a great adventure for these mountain boys, as they felt themselves protectors of the flocks: heroes.) The thin cries of girls came up to me. Laughter. Lights appeared in the doorways of the log cabins: the evening fires were being replenished. Snatches of song. Sitting there on my horse, I thought of the simple security and contentment of such an existence.

The Tartar cavalcade came up—and went on. They would not camp near these people, for some reason. And when Wicker and I rode down into the bowl and made our presence known, we thought we could understand the Tartars' reluctance. For these people were entirely different from any others we had seen in the Caucasus. In bulk, any one of them would have made two Tartars. Big-boned men, with blue eyes, with heavy blonde beards and moustaches. The same custom was observed: the knot of men asking us questions, while they made up their mind whether they would offer us a place to sleep before their fires. And then when they led us to a long cabin that had obviously just been made in shape for us, we saw women with their blonde hair done in plaits around their heads. And not wearing bloomers, as did the women of the Mohammedan tribes.

It would have been useless to speculate on their origin. But they were, more than likely, a pocket of people left from the Norsemen who founded Kiev, then went on down the Dnieper to cross the Black Sea to the Caucasus. There was not a trace of the Asiatic either in them or their customs.

It was a night that I shall never forget. That night, trying to write my notes; what it was like to sit on my horse and watch some fifty miles of snows change colours in the sunset, I knew that I just could not do it. It was only some seven or eight years later, in Paris, impelled by the wine perhaps, that I reached for a bit of paper and carefully, tenderly, savouring each word before I used it, captured the very essence of that experience. The only poem I ever wrote in my life. And then promptly tore it up.

Wicksteed was dead by then. He died alone, unattended, in his one little room in Moscow, unnoticed by the foreign colony, as he had been in life. And as it was his lovable, whimsical old character which made this trip the almost mid-Victorian adventure that it turned out to be—he was always piqued when I told him that his company reminded me of *Travels with a Donkey in the Cevennes*—perhaps I had better introduce you to him.

He was a character. Shakespeare and Dante scholar, friend of the Webbs, steadfast, even stoic believer in all that the Bolsheviks claimed for the new world they were building, he was managing to eke out a living when I got to know him by teaching English to a small class in one of Moscow's universities (Berlitz method, he claimed) by the simple process of not bothering to learn any Russian himself. This seemed to work wonderfully. His needs were few. And so that there should not be any doubts about the authenticity of his having gone Russian, he had shaved his grey head, cultivated what he thought was the appropriate professorial beard, and went about Moscow clad in a belted rubashka and knee-high stinking boots.

This did not work at all. It is queer that no one has ever stressed this *parvenu* side of the Communist character; but the Bolshevik Russians, at least in those days, only accepted a foreigner at the value which they saw his own countrymen placed upon him. The fact that he really loved the Russians, and even believed in the Bolsheviks (see Wicksteed's *Ten Years in Soviet Moscow*), cut no ice with them: they were snobs of the first water. And as by no conceivable stretch of the imagination could Alexander Wicksteed be induced to put on an orthodox Western tie and collar while in Russia (this would have been a shameful surrender to bourgeois conventions!) he was seldom, if ever, invited to the functions of the Diplomatic Corps, or even to those of the foreign press correspondents. And as these two bodies which, *faute de mieux*, had to fraternise with each other, in that alien world, were about all there was of a foreign colony in the Moscow of those days, Wicksteed was a Nobody. I think he thoroughly enjoyed it.

There were many things about Alexander Wicksteed that I didn't know. Some revelations came only years after his death. One was that he had been a missionary in Africa.

He lived in one little room (and died there) in one of Moscow's dingiest and most Dostoevsky-like tenements, over in the old working quarter. Wicker's block of buildings contained 200 rooms—in which were living 1,000 people! The house was built on the "corridor system"; that is to say, not arranged in flats, but where each single room opened out on a common corridor. A human warren, where

Dead monastery on the Volga

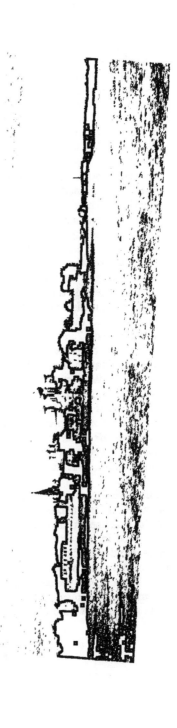

whole families lived in dingier and even dirtier single rooms on either side of him; where, if you stopped your own talk for a moment, you could hear them carrying on, as Russians still dared to do in those comparatively free days, their everlasting arguments about their souls and current politics. Or have to listen to them take their violent personal quarrels out into the dark corridor or into the greasy communal kitchen. What the communal toilet must have been like I dread to think; I found that the Russians were not yet house-broken, even when I went back there in 1941: they are, so far as disposing of their excrement goes, the dirtiest of all the animals. Wicksteed's own little room (of which he was so proud!) was a cell so jam-packed with furniture that no one could have crossed it in a straight line in any one direction. Everything that he owned in the world, in Russia at any rate, was packed in something, under some-thing, or was hanging from something. He cooked most of his own meals, such as they were, on a rusty little spirit stove, and lived on the slim rations allotted to every under-privileged citizen of Red Moscow. Centre, shrine of this Mad Hatter's castle, was an immense brass samovar, around which he had fondly imagined great philo-sophical discussions would be held. But the little hard chairs around the table were usually empty. And as Wicker, who fancied himself as a handyman, had made his two alleged easy chairs himself, and as it was as much as your manhood was worth to risk sitting down on them, I always took the bed. There during many a snowy night in the cold winter of 1928–29, I lay and listened to old Wicksteed talk about the Caucasus—"Ah, they are 'a land of water wet, grass green, and mountains steep.' "

They were his dream. He had come into Russia with the Quaker Relief during the terrible Volga famine of 1921–22. At one time he had two sections of the lower Volga under his food control; as large as all Middlesex. He had known many Russians, made many good friends. But one by one these had all slipped, or been scared, away from him. And now he had a hankering, a lust, to get back to the country itself, the very land of old Russia—the soil, the streams, the forests, the mountains; and the more untainted by man they were, the better. So every year now when his course in the Moscow univer-sity closed in May, he packed his camp kit, took his staff, and with such small money and provisions as he had been able to lay by during the winter, he lit out for the Caucasus. He usually made for the

Teberda river, in the Karachaite country. There he found a tree, took out his sonnets, and lay down under it. Thus passed a summer. . . .

The one visitor who could be found almost every evening in Wicksteed's room was a youth named Peter, ingenuous to the point of being mental; a former pupil of Wicker's, who had attached himself as a sort of Kim to his beloved professor. I learned a lot about Russians from him; the world that the young Russians still saw in prospect. Many a night I wandered through the back streets of Moscow listening to his naïveté; or went to the Park of Culture and Rest, to the shooting gallery, where I shot the monocle out of Austen Chamberlain's eye. Peter was young, enthusiastic, and absolutely certain he was right. But he was harmless.

Perhaps Peter was not such a dolt as he seemed. One night when I got as far as asking him if he did not mind the fear—always present in any Soviet Russian's mind—of living under the constant eyes of the G.P.U., Peter frowned and was silent. Then he said thoughtfully: "*Da!* I do. But you must understand that it is *our* Russia they are watching over." (There it was: always "*Our* Russia; all this is *ours!*" Even a prisoner in chains feels this supreme love for Russia; as if the land itself would win through in the long run, and set him free—it is his undying illusion).

The other Russian visitor to Wicker's room, who defied secret police scrutiny, was of a macabrely different sort. A grim, pale-faced engineer, a sort of Grand Guignol character, who always made me feel uneasy: it was enough to chill anyone, to see the way he always peered up and down the dark corridor, before he softly closed Wicksteed's door behind him. He detested the garrulous Peter, and when he was there would sit for the whole evening, speaking only to say "Thanks" as Wicker filled his glass of tea for him. He always gave me the unhappy impression that, like so many Russians of that time, he knew his days were numbered. They were: he was liquidated that spring while Wicker and I were in the Caucasus. When last heard of he was a prisoner in the Solovietsky Monastery up on the White Sea. Yet he was the one who was really responsible for our trip. I had an old 1914 Russian Baedeker, and had brought it along one night so that Wicksteed could mark for me some of the places he had been to in case I could make another trip to the Caucasus. This engineer had been on a geodetic survey of the Caucasus; and at the sight of the maps his face completely changed. He studied them while Wicker rambled on about the land of "grass green, mountains steep", then he took his pencil out and marked the region leading to Mt. Elbruz. "If you go in there," he said, tracing a line from Kislovodsk, "you will find that 'they' [the Communists] have not yet got much above 5,000 feet There you will find the Caucasus as they used to be—the home of absolutely free men! And men of a fierce freedom such as you will find nowhere else in the world. This part of Russia is like the North-West Frontier of India—and its tribesmen are as wild as the Afridis." He sighed. "At any rate—they *were*." He said that if Wicker, who had never made this approach from the eastern side, walked at an altitude of 7,000 to 8,000 feet, he could easily wade the streams, which were fordable at that height. He could live with the mountain shepherds over most of the distance. And he would even find one or two valleys in which no one lived at all. "Anyway, they were deserted when I was there. Why, I don't know. Tribal fights, probably." And he began to describe mountain streams and forests that were a paradise on earth.

Wicker listened impatiently. "Deserted valleys—eh?" he finally managed to break in. "Well!—will you please tell me one thing! Where would I get my *food*?"

"We could take horses," I said. "*We*?" gasped old Wicker, his brown eyes lighting up. "Do you mean it?"

I told him that I had never meant anything more. The minute the engineer began to talk about that part of the high Caucasus, where arrogant Communism had not yet been able to establish its irritating sway, I knew that I was going to go there. "I'd like to see what the life is like there," I told him. "I can get my paper to pay for it. They must be tired of my always writing about politics, and that damned Five Year Plan. I'll wire them tomorrow morning, suggest a horse-back ride into the remote Caucasus: 'Strange people in strange places'—something like that." We finished off Wicker's vodka that night; the engineer talked his head off; and I got an immediate reply to my cable—EXCELLENT YOUR SUGGESTION HAS GREAT SYNDICATION VALUE PROCEED.

*　　*　　*

I was part author of a play that was to be produced at the Globe in London, tail end of that winter, and I had already been given permission by my generous paper, with full expenses paid, to come out and see my own First Night. It will probably be the only one. Of the play I have nothing more to say, other than that I do not wish it robbed of its one distinction: it was, without a doubt, not only the worst play that has ever been produced but that has ever been written. The woman with whom I collaborated (it was her plot) changed my dialogue while I was in Russia, inserting one gem of her own: to wit—"*White* men don't run!" This had to be said seriously, by Raymond Massey. It almost killed him. On the second night, in the middle of the second act, I reached under the seat, took my hat, and went back to Moscow.

But before that, during the play's stormy rehearsals, I had bought one of the finest camp kits for our trip through the Caucasus that Fortnum and Mason could supply. And when it came to food I did us both proud. This was 1929, before the New York Stock Exchange crashed; and foreign correspondents' expense accounts were counted nothing—provided you sent good stories to justify them. We lived like little rajahs. Embittered by my flop as a playwright, I resolved that the Caucasian journey was going to be a success, even if my expense account made our foreign editor howl. Prize purchases were two bed-rolls with two rubberised groundsheets, out of which I had already invented a quickly erected pup-tent for old Wicker and myself. It gave us good shelter on many a night during the rain or the hail storms of the high Caucasus. And then, as we had decided that our main diet would be from mountain sheep we could buy from the shepherds, I had two waxed-cloth bags made, large enough to hold a leg of lamb each. This to prevent the flies from blowing the meat. Other waxed bags were made for rice, etc.; a complete folding cooking outfit of aluminium utensils. Then with a duffle-bag full of tea, coffee, tins of jam, etc.—most of them unobtainable in Russia—1,000 Gold Flake cigarettes in tins, and my favourite trout rod, I arrived back in Moscow.

* * *

Old Wicksteed had had many a meal with me in my two rooms in the Grand Hotel. But never a dinner half so jolly as the one we had that night with a couple of bottles of that sweet Crimean wine that goes by the name of champagne. I spread the loot from London out on the floor. Wicker was flabbergasted. "But *that*," he said finally, as if glad to be able to find something that he could refuse, "that I shall *not* need." He jabbed his pipe at the bed-roll and Jaeger flea-bag.

"No? Got a better one?"

"No. Just a special one. Made it myself."

While in London, as I had a friend in the Lister Institute who did it free, I had had myself inoculated against every affliction I could think of. The reason was that I had spent eight months out of the year 1927–28 in bed, recovering from a severe bone operation on my foot. I had got out of plaster only just before I returned for a year in Russia; the wound was still open—I was forced to wear a felt surgical boot—and I did not want to take any chances. One of our two horses was to be for me, the other our pack animal. Wicker, as I have said, was determined to walk the whole distance.

"I will go at just such-and-such a pace," he said, getting up and slowly pacing the carpet of my room. "No faster, no slower. Gravity notwithstanding. Up hill, down hill—on the flat. You will see!" he said, slumping back in my chair, flinging one smelly knee-high boot over the other. "Nothing will make me change it. Why—I've walked the legs off these Karachaites many a time!"

He could. I saw him do it. I had also bought a plentiful supply of flowers of sulphur while in London. I had found it a blessing on a mule-ride I made through Spain, sleeping in the muleteers' *fondas*. But Wicker refused it: he would not "coat himself" with that yellow insecticide. "Then eat it!" I laughed. "It won't hurt you. You will sweat it through your pores—as I've done many a time—and no bug will touch you."

Wicker said that despite bugs, and rationing difficulties in Moscow, he was not going to begin our trip by eating sulphur. Then he told me, with great glee, that he had managed to collect nearly a whole kilo of tea during the winter. He did this by trading his tea leaves with the other inhabitants of his human warren. The deal was that for four parts of his—once used—he received one part of fresh tea leaves from them. Of course, they had to take his word for it that his had been only once used. But then, Alexander Wicksteed was an English gentleman. And somehow, in all that gruesome slum, he managed to make the other people know it.

* * *

The winter of 1928–29 was unquestionably the high point of the

Russian Revolution. Never since has the dream of 1917, of the Old Bolsheviki, looked so near to being realised. The Russians were still human (as they will be again some day). You could still travel about Russia and talk to strange people without fear of their being terrified, especially those you might meet in a train or on a boat—always accepting the probability, of course, that the friendly little blonde, who asked such naïve questions, had been deliberately planted on you by the G.P.U. Even so, looking back on it, the dreaded G.P.U. was really a grandfatherly organisation compared to its successor, the N.K.V.D. You could still go to a railway station and buy a ticket for nearly any part of Russia, in that year I spent under the Soviets between September 1928 and September 1929, without having to get permission from the Foreign Office or even telling your girl secretary where you intended to go. You just went. That was such a normal state of affairs, under the dictatorship of the proletariat, that it bewildered the group of American newspapers which employed me; so much so that some of the editors even refused to believe it. And Soviet Russians born around that date could hardly believe today such freedom to go where you wanted!

This was the winter of the first year of the First Five Year Plan. That detestable organisation the secret police was still devoting its persecution to the comparative few, rather than the millions they began to kill or send to slave labour camps in the forced collectivisation of the farms which began the next spring. (In September 1929 Paul Scheffer, of the *Berliner Tageblatt*, and I went down on the Don steppes, and wrote the first eyewitness stories of the brutal forced collectivisation of the farms. That was when my faith in the 1917 Revolution, which I had witnessed, began to die.) N.E.P., the right to small private trading which Lenin had reinstated in 1922, had not yet been quite abolished—a little shop in the Hunter's Market behind our hotel sold us all the fine grey Caspian caviare, smoked Volga fish, and sweet Caucasian wine that anybody could desire; and the Soviet Theatre was in full, glorious blossom. Before its petals began to fall, under the frost of ideological censorship, and it still looked as if the Communist bosses were going to respect genius above everything else, we saw—that wonderful winter, when Red Moscow seemed the most exhilarating capital I had ever been in—Moskvin and Knipper-Chekova (Chekov's wife) play their original parts in *The Cherry Orchard*; at the Thirtieth Anniversary of the incomparable little Art Theatre we saw the great Stanislavsky play, for one act, the rôle he had originally made world-famous in *The Three Sisters*, and one act of Moskvin playing in *The Brothers Karamazov*; we saw Kachalov's "green" *Hamlet* (unquestionably the gloomiest Dane that ever trod the boards); we saw *Boris Gudunov*, given as a straight play by the Art Theatre, where realism went to the extent of actually taking the costumes of the period from Moscow's Historical Museum, and a young bass sang Boris with a power, so all the Bolshies said, that made even the great Chaliapin sound like an amateur. (Though not to any Westerner who had ever heard Chaliapin). I met Stanislavsky.

It was a winter of sensual delight; there is no other way to describe it. And on that peak of the Revolution, between the glorious intoxicating promise of 1917 and the slave-state that Russia has become today, when the more fiery among the young Communists were bent on making new rules for everything, morals in particular, the story went around Moscow that a dozen startlingly beautiful young girls had boarded a tramcar stark naked—except for a narrow ribbon across their pretty stomachs, bearing the challenge : *"Only the malformed need wear clothes."* I missed that: but, as I have tried to make clear, it was a thrilling winter—full of great expectations. I wandered, freely, all over European Russia in the year I spent there in 1928–29.

* * *

And so it came that, one sunny afternoon in May, when I was sitting on my window-sill watching the Chinese jugglers, in their blue coolie cloth, entertaining the Soviet children below the pink walls of the Kremlin, the 'phone rang.

"Farson? Wicksteed speaking. Are you there? Well!—are you ready, Farson?"

"Ready—aye, ready! What time do we sail?"

"Six o'clock. . . . I think I've almost got the tickets."

"What do you mean by *almost*?"

"Well—ah—Peter went off to fetch them, and—ah—I haven't seen him all day. I suggest that it would be better to come along. I'll meet you there: *Ustinski Most*—that's the second bridge below the Kremlin. . . ."

"Yes, yes; I know. But what is the name of the boat?"

"It has none."

That was Wicker. I found the boat. A tiny little paddle-wheeler, with a low, flat upper deck to allow her to get under bridges. She looked like a flat-iron. There was the inevitable motley mob of peasants and proletarians, all fighting to get aboard her at the same time. An apathetic few were sitting on their mounds of three-ply yellow suitcases and bundles, while the children—that one form of production at which the Russians seem really efficient—climbed over the mountains of luggage, screamed, giggled, fought, and almost fell into the river as they hopped up and down trying to dance to a tinkling little folk song that a one-eyed ragged minstrel was playing on his accordion. Spring was certainly in the air. . . .

Then, at last, came old Wicksteed—very much the "professor". Grey beard and shaven head, disdainful as ever of a necktie; his shirt open, sandals on his feet, but, lo!—dressed in a well-cut Scottish tweed and a not too badly pressed pair of flannel bags. He was blowing great puffs of blue smoke from the stinking *mahorka* (that peasant substitute for real tobacco) that filled his contented pipe. There was a studied languor in his gait, in the casual way he was letting Peter carry both his heavy rucksacks—in the way he walked straight through that fighting crowd and on to the boat, never slacking his progress.

"Why on earth did you wear that get-up?" I asked him, as we stowed our stuff in our cabin. "On this day of all days!"—for this was the first time I had seen him in an English costume.

"There are occasions," he rejoined, "when one must be what one is. This day is one of them. You saw how it worked."

He seemed to crave his own company when first he got aboard. Standing up forward, gazing down river. His work at the Moscow university was over for the summer. No more students. He was free!

At six o'clock the steamer gave a hoarse shriek and cast off. We began to slip under the bridges—the last we would pass under before we were forcibly driven inside our closed cabins for fear we would hang bombs on these main Russian arteries. The river went out into the country and then wound back again. It seemed unable, somehow, to get loose from Moscow. And Moscow, in the green sunset, became a fantastic outline of turbaned church domes and towers in black silhouette. The golden dome of the Semenovsky monastery again appeared on our bows. Its Muscovite tower still held the black eagle of the Romanovs. It looked like a startled scarecrow.

· 36 ·

Every man in this photo is dead—shot on the spot—or was sent to Siberia when Stalin deported these freedom loving tribes from their native Caucasus Khassaut

And behind it, rising high against the green sky, was the haystack mast of the Third Internationale wireless station. I called Wicker's attention to the lesson which these two "towers of truth" might hold for the thoughtful man. Suddenly, he became active, patting himself all over.

"Damn!—oh, damn!—oh, damn!" he swore. "I can't see! I can't even *see*!—I've forgotten my long-distance spectacles!"

* * *

The little Moscow river was shallow, hardly more than a creek; though it was the small stream on which Peter the Great built his first boat, before he came to England to work as a shipwright. Our little flat-iron was called *Thanks*; and her red-faced skipper was, most unideologically, not a good Comrade. When, the next morning, we found ourselves stymied by an immense wood-barge which had insolently anchored out in mid-channel, and whose jeering crew refused to move her, our captain called for full-steam, jammed himself between the bank and the wood-barge; and used *Thanks* as a wedge. The planks of the barge began to crack; her crew screamed, we grinned; *Thanks* herself was tilted and shoved up on the bank, her right paddles clipping the weeds like a lawn-mower; and we squeezed through. Our captain looked back at the holed barge with a smile which seemed to say: this is a proletarian country where all men may be equal—but not ships! His feat got a tip of the hat from the captain of a big tug from the Caspian, lying with her oil-barge in a fairly wide stretch down below. The sight of that big barge from Baku, 2,500 miles away, was like meeting a whale in the immense emptiness of that grassy plain.

II

IF it should strike anyone as strange that we *sailed* from Moscow,
then let me say that for the first 700 miles we followed the same
rivers that took Ivan the Terrible to his conquest of Kazan: 115
miles down the little Moskva to Ryazan; 550 miles down the Oka
to Nijni-Novgorod; 1,100 miles down the broad and shining Volga
to Stalingrad. Nearly 1,800 miles of slow river travel in Russia, with
all the lazy languor that implied. Then there would be 500 miles
across the Don and Kuban steppes—until 60 miles off, we would see
the white cone of Mt. Elbruz begin to rise over the green plain. We
would travel 2,300 miles before we even touched a horse.

There were days on those long river trips that I shall always
remember. Complete peace. The tensions of Moscow lay behind us.
The ship seemed to paddle on for ever under its great bowl of blue
sky. The ice had gone, and the steppes, which had lain locked in snow
for the six winter months, were now sweeps of green to the far
horizon. They were flowered. Islands of that yellow bloom that the
Russians call " chicken blind" seemed to float on the sunny grass.
Clumps of cattle and horses, grazing in the far distance, stood up
like other islands. On nearly all the rivers of European Russia the
right bank is high and the left low: the Hill Bank and the Meadow
Bank, the Russians call them. The right bank is hilly and raw, red
sandstone, or clay bluffs, with occasional forests of jagged pine on
its rim. A cold, northern aspect. One had continually to remind oneself that this country is on the latitude of Hudson Bay. On the left is
the interminable tableland: flat grassy plains, with not a bush on
them, or low meadows with thickets of willows. A dark line along
the willows, about twenty feet above the river, shows where
the recent high water has been. Below that line the trees are
dark and without any leaves. Above it they are billows of bright
green.

Two weeks ago this tableland and meadow were completely under water, and the Oka was often twenty miles wide. Only the tips of the trees showed above it. Up here, when the ice breaks, the Oka rises forty-five feet.

It is a lonely river. Yet there are churches and minarets along it that were old long before Columbus set sail for the Americas. It is still primitive. We round a bend and come on two fishermen. They are out in their narrow black dugouts, sculling their aboriginal craft with one hand. Skiffs cut from one log. Even from the deck of our passing steamer I could see the flake marks of the small adze. They use a paddle somewhat like the American Indian's—but cupped like a spoon. They move in pairs across the lonely water, and they have a net slung between them. As we pass, I stare; for in the bottom of one dugout lies a long-snouted water monster that must be over four feet long. A sturgeon? Very likely: they come far up these rivers to spawn.

The banks of the Oka are gouged raw by the spring ice. Yet the cliff swallows have already bored their nests in them. They skim out from the upper strata and sail dizzily ahead of our pushing bows. I lean forward and try to grasp the colours of the morning: the blinding sheen of the waves as we turn toward the rising sun, the wet green of the tableland, the faint blues of the distance, the fawn of sandbars wet with the night dew. Jacksnipe and sandpipers feed and flit along the cold river edge. Ducks beat up from hidden reaches and whistle down the sky. This is a high enough latitude for them to rest for the summer, end their migration, and raise their young. Although, high in the sky, we still saw strings of wild geese pushing north. The spring floods have left a number of small pools in the grassy meadows. Mallard and teal rise out of them as our ship comes along. A yellow ribbon of road leads to a peasant village. . . .

This is a scene that might have come straight out of Turgenev's *Sportsman's Sketches*. The log huts of the village lie on the rim and folds of a dark ravine. As the paddles stop and the ship slides ahead I can hear the cocks crowing and the chirping and trilling of birds in the little orchards along the shore. The lonely village seems asleep. Yet from some of the thatched roofs drifts the smoke of early fires. Our ship makes fast. A few peasants get off, their legs wrapped in cloth and birchbark shoes. Among them is a girl in city clothes. She is met by an old woman in a red skirt, bare-legged, with a white kerchief over her head. A young man kisses the girl awkwardly and walks with her wooden suitcases as they go up to the log blockhouses. Local stevedores, with leather saddles on their backs, trot in and out of the ship. They stagger out, a long line of them, swinging their arms loosely to keep their balance, under heavy boxes and bales, iron sheets, rolls of tar-paper, crates of galvanised buckets, iron kettles—and a brightly painted reaper. Peasant carts are lined up on the shore, their drivers in high conical sheepskin hats, their beards unkempt, their long yellow hair cut square at the neck like a fringe of straw. One peasant goes from cart to cart, sliding off the broad-hubbed wheels until they are just held up by the axle-tip; then he swabs the wooden axle with a wad of tar. Atop one cart climbs a young engineer from our ship, with a hammer and anchor on his visored cap; and on top of his luggage he places his guitar—to cheer him in his exile. The ship goes on. We see bare-footed peasants, in their scarlet *rubashkas*, following the plough. Women and girls, in long lines, bent over, setting young plants. The river ahead is broad and lazy blue and sandbars glisten in the sun. We slip past the rose towers and yellow walls of a monastery, round a white buoy, and paddle farther into Central Russia.

We lay over at Ryazan most of one day, taking on a cargo of vodka that our ship was going to trade for little pigs all the way down the Oka. Crates of vodka for crates of squealing and very loose-bowelled little pigs. The town lay about a mile back from the river at this time of the year, with the water falling. Some cerise church towers lured us into it. You have to read a lot of Chekov to understand a town like Ryazan, and you have to know a few towns like Ryazan to understand Chekov—why, some of even his most ardent admirers will weakly admit that he had a flair for dullness. No man ever gave a truer picture of the drabness of Russian provincial life. The boredom of these little Russian country towns must have been phenomenal. It seizes you by the throat. You stare at the dilapidated plaster buildings around you, at the empty cobbled squares, at the one or two grandiose Empire-style residences of the aristocracy, and your soul is filled with gloom.

You wonder as you stare into the dusty droning stores if the clerks there go home to luncheon; if in the summer they eat their lunch behind closed blinds—and with what weariness they must have come out into the sun glare of the streets to resume their ordeal in the shop. There seems no life there.

Your mind pictures darkened rooms behind those blinds of faded slats. You understand now why such inconsolable habitations, so shut off from universal life, have produced such exotic and brilliant minds. You understand Stefan Trofimovitch of *The Possessed*; and *The Brothers Karamazov*. Merely to think, to live in the realm of the mind, is escape from the town, even if it is into a world of self-induced madness. For the more easily satisfied and less tortured there was always, of course, Market Day, the Horse Fair, billiards at the Club; the regiments passing through on their summer manœuvres, with the dashing young officers calling on their old colonels—especially those who had pretty daughters. And there were those Russian girls (how lovely they were!) laughing and twittering like little birds as they packed hampers for a picnic by the cool river. . . . Now all that was gone. The life of this town had been scooped out. It was an empty shell. A vulgar cemetery. And after lurching a while through its pitted streets, in which our *isvostchik* and his old horse seemed the only things left of the old régime, we told our driver to take us quickly back to the boat There old Wicksteed gave his verdict.

"Nothing!" he said bitterly. "Nothing but unmitigated and incessant vice could make life in that town even bearable!"

We had hardly cast loose from the shore before he began to make friends. And such friends. First, let me say that when a Russian gets aboard a train, or a boat—anything moving—he instantly becomes a different person. He sheds restrictions, fears, inhibitions, just as easily and automatically as a snake sheds his skin. He says things that would get him in prison on *terra firma*, even shot. Nothing can stop him from saying them, even when he can see that you do not want to listen. This, it can be said safely, was true of all Russians, rich or poor—up until the time when the Police State finally achieved its dehumanising task of making them a nation of robots; which, I would say, had been fatally accomplished by 1936: the Russia which automatically cheered the murders of the Great Purge. It was not by accident that Tolstoy staged *The Kreutzer Sonata* in a railway train. That terrible tale of an unresolved lover-hate, so acutely anticipating modern psycho-analysis, where one passenger forces another, a total stranger, to listen to his tale of self-accusation, his own wretched character; and how he murdered his wife. Such a confession becomes not at all out of the ordinary, when it is told in the sleeping compartment of a Russian railway carriage. And this, be it remembered, was in the comparatively free year of 1929.

I found Wicksteed in the dining saloon for the first-class passengers; not quite the centre, yet securely an active member of a congenial little coterie consisting of an ex-*bez prizorney*, an Instructor in Communism, a young engineering student from Leningrad who was studying to become a professor, and an indescribably ugly but happy little Tartar with a rose-embroidered skull cap who, we were to learn, played the guitar all day long. The *bez prizorney* was a reformed ragamuffin, one of those waifs of the Revolution, or of the famines, whom the G.P.U. were pursuing and catching all over Soviet Russia—usually in the cellars or ruins of abandoned houses, where they were living with young girls, equally wild, and mostly syphilitic. Wicksteed got it out of this one that he had wandered away from his home on the Volga during the 1921 famine, and was being sent back. He already knew that his parents were dead; yet he was a happy little chap, full of great expectations for the new life that was before him. No doubt he has grown up to be a big Bolshevik now, hating all foreigners like poison.

Jeunesse Dorée, for that was what we came to call the Instructor in Communism, was startling. He had, presumably, come abroad dressed in ordinary clothes. But once he had made sure that Ryazan was left safely behind, and that we would not hit another town of any size for over 550 miles, he dashed into his cabin and reappeared in a costume of dazzling white. White duck trousers, white canvas shoes, white silk *rubashka* belted with a silver tassel, with a white wand-like walking stick which had a silver knob. Atop all this was, believe it or not, a white yachting cap. Where he had got it all, in Soviet Russia, was beyond comprehension. He was going down into one of the backward Volga republics, he informed us. He must have been a surprise.

"But he must be a very brave man," said old Wicker. "In Moscow, they'd shoot a Communist for wearing a get-up like that. If he really is a Communist. . . . I'm afraid *Jeunesse Dorée* is headed for a very sticky end."

Like most good proletarian ships, we carried four classes: 63 people above decks, 584 below. First and second slept in comfortable cabins on the saloon deck, and had their own dining saloons. Third and fourth, a class known as "deckers," slept between decks—with the cargo. And as the cargo on the Oka at this time of the spring became more and more these crates of jittery little pigs, I, for one, fully appreciated class distinctions. So did a peasant I found sleeping on a bed of factory pulleys. He looked like a bear, with his grisly black beard and green sheepskin coat with the wool-side turned in— a bear who liked vodka. He told me that he was going to Astrakhan, at the same time admitting that he hadn't the faintest idea why, or what he was going to do when he got there. "It doesn't matter," he said—his ticket from Nijni-Novgorod to Astrakhan, travelling "decker" as he was, cost him only the equivalent of sixteen shillings for 1,500 miles.

He belched grandly and pointed his huge paw at a swarm of other peasants who were listening, awed, to the voice of a Communist Commissar talking to them from Moscow over the radio—all the wonders of the New Life. "Listen!" he said. "Did you ever hear such——! *Before*—when they lied to us—they had to do it to our faces. Now—they can stay in Moscow—and lie to us *with that!*"

Our first morning on the Oka was largely given over to the search for old Wicker's long-distance spectacles. He had to unpack all his kit. And I was made to examine and appreciate every bit of it. He had two revolutionary rucksacks, with twisted straps, which had seen seven years of Russia and several thousand weary miles. They were filled with cheese, butter, hardware, and gadgets. He produced a rusty tin canister. "I call that very useful," he said. Inside it was his bath sponge. "This is sugar," he said, bringing out a blue sewing-bag. "And this is cheese"—another blue sewing-bag. "I wash these bags," he remarked, catching my startled stare—"that is, when I think they need it." Butter was found in an old caviare tin, in which (he couldn't think how it got there) there was also a ham sandwich. Quite gaseous.

We had a long way to go, a couple of thousand miles or so; and we weren't at all sure how we were going to live, or with whom, when we got there. He held up a gigantic blue porcelain flask. "*This!* . . . This is for vodka . . . sort of courteous return, y'know, for any people we might stop with." The mountaineers of the Caucasus were very hospitable, he said—but peculiar. He stared at the flask longingly. It was empty. Another flask, aluminium, held the spirits for his little cooking-stove. And his bed-roll, made for him by a female admirer ("Clever woman, that—always trying to marry me"), was a patchwork quilt—unwashable and unwashed—folded over like an omelette, and sewn to a light kapok mattress. I had brought along the elegant bed-roll and flea-bag that I had bought for him at Fortnum and Mason's, despite his rejection of it; but in the high Caucasus, on some of the coldest nights, I envied old Wicker on his kapok mattress. Cold can hit you from below, you know. In fact, after vetting his whole outfit carefully, the only thing I could suggest throwing away, and I did it quite firmly, was the caviare tin of butter, which was already quite terrifying.

"You can't insult me," he said, looking up. "If you think that I need a bath you may say so. I won't feel offended. I only take insults when I am sure they are meant. And in that case you will have to be very pointed and specific about it."

"I'll try to think of something," I said.

I had a big duffle-bag, too big, a small suitcase, and my little Corona typewriter. And the two bed-rolls. I know of nothing more unintended to be put on a horse than a duffle-bag. Especially when it is full. This one held my clothes, the collapsible aluminium cooking kit, the few books I was taking, and about eight hundred Gold Flake cigarettes, in tins of fifty. None of it could be jettisoned. We had agreed to travel light, and a compromise had to be found between his kit and mine, with some surrenders. We were afraid we had too much for one pack-horse. Not the weight, but the bulkiness of it all. We were afraid, and we were right, that the bulging load might push the horse off the trail, especially on some of the narrow ledges going around the spurs. Yet we had these 2,300 miles to go before we had to worry about how we would pack our horses. And we discussed our compromise with no sense of urgency. Talks conducted with continual tea-drinking. This Wicksteed made by going down to the engine room and drawing a kettleful of boiling water from the *kipyatok*, the hot-water tap. Then he doused an aluminium tea-egg in our filled glasses. When the chain of this gadget broke and I was wondering how we would get it out, he instantly whipped a pair of mechanic's pliers from the back pocket of his shorts. "I *never* travel without these," he announced, handing me the pliers to admire. His shorts had been made by amputating the legs of a pair of pin-stripe trousers. Though where he would ever have worn a morning suit, except lecturing on Russia to some Society of Cultural Relations in England, I cannot say. I understood, however, that he was always

· 44 ·

in great demand by the Fabians when he came home, as he would be. He had probably bought these astonishing trousers, as a bargain, from one of those pathetic old curiosity shops which still shook the hearts of foreigners visiting Leningrad or Moscow: shops where they sold old tinkling music boxes, former uniforms, top hats and opera cloaks—relics of a life that was never to return.

"Do you like salt?" he said, holding up another rusty canister.

"Of course. Why not?"

"Well, I do. It adds another day to the life of your meat."

Lest anyone may think there was something boy-scoutish about this eccentric old gentleman's addiction to shorts, rucksacks, and walking trips, let me say that during the 1914–18 war Wicksteed had been a coal-heaver in a mine-sweeper. He had been a conscientious objector; but, as he put it, "I just couldn't sit on my arse, in a posh job, while I saw that better men than I ever hope to be were getting killed," and "I *liked* the life . . . real, downright, good-hearted chaps. And besides, ever since I was the age of fifteen, I have been trying to liquidate my class pretensions." Then he made the neat and very disarming confession: "But, do you know—even in that Grimsby trawler, the men said I was dirty!"

Our meals in the first- and second-class dining saloon were rather chancy. The ship carried two cooks, but as one of them disappeared the first night—whether overside or not, no one knew—the other cook, whose day off it was supposed to be, refused to cook at all. We did not mind so much: my first *table d'hôte* meal on the *Dekabrist*, which without looking at the menu I told the waiter to bring me, turned out to be (it was breakfast) iced radishes and cold potatoes. And having placed the dishes on our table the steward disappeared some place where neither I nor anyone else could find him. We thus took to cooking our own meals. The one art, as it happened, that old Wicker had been secretly aching to demonstrate. "You just leave this to me!" he said. "If you'll just let me have the cabin to myself?"

Wicker's attitude toward the few meals we did eat in the disgusting dining saloon savoured of the stoic. I refused to eat the *cotelettes*, the dubious-looking meat-balls, which, I noticed, were served as the main dish for the meal directly following a recognisable meat course. "They are made up of what people leave on their plates," I told Wicksteed. "I dare say," he replied, munching placidly—"but sometimes they leave the nice bits."

As I have said, the third-class and the "deckers" on our proletarian ship had no restaurant, and had to forage for themselves. This food was provided by the peasants who stood in two lines on the bank at each landing place. They sold milk, hard-boiled (and unwashed) eggs, onions, bread, and little fish out of the very frying pans they were cooked in. At every landing the third and fourth-class charged up the gang-plank. Wicker joined the stampede. Here, he was wise enough to know, it also paid to look like a foreigner: you got the best pickings. And I could see him, his bald head shining in the sun, the centre of a crowding little scrum of peasant girls, calmly selecting what he wanted. He came back with fish, once with two smoked *sigi*, that delectable golden fish with a wooden plug in its mouth; he bought beautiful fresh butter, at one place shaped in little pine cones; and always, for he loved making *omelette confiture*—I had opened a tin of apricot jam for him—he came back with my green canvas water-bucket full of eggs. "Just leave it to me," he would say earnestly. "But I must have the cabin to myself!" He was a prodigious eater, when he got the chance; and we averaged four meals a day. When one was ready he would find me on the deck, bow, and say with ill-concealed satisfaction: "The Ambassador is served."

Well—I began to notice things. I couldn't help it. And one day, after I had finished a real masterpiece of my *cordon bleu*—he had used a dozen eggs to make a mushroom omelette, as well as my only clean face-towel for a tablecloth—I lay there in my bunk, wondering if the time had come when I really must say something. That something specific that old Wicker had warned me about. "You can't insult *me*," he had said. Now, unsuspecting, filled with the triumph of achievement, he sat there, swinging his legs on his bunk. "If you'll just give me one of your beastly cigarettes," he said, lazily getting to his feet, "I'll begin to clean up and take these things down to the hot-water tap." He picked up the frying pan.

"Wicker," I said, "I've been thinking. I think I'll get off at Nijni, cross the river—and take the train straight from there to the Caucasus. I'll meet you at Kislovodsk. Have the horses by the time you get there."

He collapsed. "Will you?" he said dolefully, from the edge of his bunk. "How? There is no train, you know, from the other side of the Volga to the Caucasus. The only train, from Nijni, goes straight back to Moscow. What's the matter? What have I done?"

"Look under your bunk." He had thrown the dozen egg-shells there. I had seen them, from where I had been lying on my side smoking. Not only that, I had seen other egg-shells. Even fish-heads. Remains of the *sigi* and from other triumphs. I now sat up, having gone this far, and (distastefully) pulled his handkerchief off our block of butter. "Do you see this?" I asked.

He coughed. "That handkerchief," he said hoarsely, giving a tug at his beard. "I suppose you know the principle of evaporation? The air passing over that wet handkerchief cools the butter. And ——"

"But you'd *used* it!" I cried angrily.

He didn't say anything. He got down on his knees, peered under his bunk. He began to rake things. . . . I got up. "I'm sorry," I said, as I stood in the door, "but you told me to be specific."

I have seldom felt so ashamed of myself. There he was, on his knees. . . . I felt sick. I wandered around the deck, wondering how I could make it up to him. Finally, I had the courage to return to our cabin. He was lying in his bunk, face to the wall. I lay back in mine, picked up *The Cossacks*, and tried to read. Finally, I forgot Wicker; then—

"A-*ha*!" I heard him cry. "So—*that's* the lesson, is it?"

I sat up. Wicker's face wore a smile, but there was the triumph of a worm turned behind it.

"So that's it, is it? That *you* should substitute your cigarette ash— *look* at that table! look at the *floor*!—for my *Shakespeare*!"

I reached out and took his hand. In such ways are undying friend-ships made. "Wicker—I'll go with you. Even to hell. Dirty as you are!" And that settled it. Or so I thought.

The Oka is a romantic river and its pine-clad right bank presents one of the most melancholic skylines I have ever looked at. This mood was occasioned in me by a line of little grey Tartar mosques. Their minarets, seen against the pale green sky of the northern nights, seemed like old arms held up in warning; a reminder, a reproach that we did not kneel and strike our heads thrice to the ground in obeisance to the epoch of barbaric splendour which they represented. For they were the last of the Golden Horde, the western-most fringe of the Tartars which had rolled out of Asia—the last of Genghis Khan.

Some of the Horde had gone south after they had ridden their horses from the far-off Amur—and it was they who caused such a stir in my memory when I saw these minarets on the Oka; for, in the spring of 1915, I had visited the palace of the Khans at Bakhtchi Sarai (when I was flying, strictly as ballast, with the young Tsarist naval officers of the Black Sea fleet); and I had never quite got over my wonder at that bizarre, barbaric civilisation of those slant-eyed men and bloomered women in the flowered Crimea.* Some of the Horde had preferred to retain the wild open life of the steppe: the Kalmucks, and the Nogaï, half-naked little bowmen, who were eventually almost enslaved by the Cossacks. But the northern wing of the Golden Horde, the Tartars who most frequently raided Moscow—and built these beautiful, nostalgic mosques, with their carvings from the Koran—were the most highly advanced horsemen of the Golden Horde, who built the wonderful city of Kazan. A city on the Volga rivalling in its splendour the enamelled domes of Samarkand.

If you will look at a map of Russia you will see that Moscow lies in a great fork, made by the Volga, which rises west and south of Moscow, and the little Oka, which flows north-north-east to get up into the Volga. It was into this fork of wooded steppe that the Western Slavs first paddled their canoes, down the rivers and through the lake region of Novgorod, as hunter-trapper-settlers— always in search of furs; just as the Canadian *voyageurs* had opened up the American north-west—and Yury Dolgoruky, Prince of Suzdal, built a wooden rampart (called in Tartar, *kreml*) on the slight hill where the present Kremlin of Moscow now stands. The first church built there was called "Our Saviour in the Wood." This was in or about 1147. Then Genghis Khan and his horde of Tartars rolled out of Asia, burning and slaughtering to the gates of Kiev. They burned Moscow to the ground in 1237, slaying all the adults, taking away the children to be sold into slavery. Moscow rose from its ashes, became an appanage of the northern princedom of Novgorod; and fifty years later the Tartars destroyed it again. The third time it was rebuilt it was by permission of the Tartars, and Moscow became a Tartar protectorate. And for the next two centuries the Tartars of Kazan used the Grand Dukes of Moscow as tax collectors. But they never settled west of the Oka.

* These Crimean Tartars were all removed to Siberia after the last war. The Kremlin claims they sided with the occupying Germans.

It is a gory story, some of the bloodiest pages of all history; but it is the very core of the modern Russian: his subconsciousness. "Scratch a Russian and you will find a Tartar." It was the Tartars who taught the Slav Russians their ferocity. The high whining note in the music of Rimsky-Korsakov is the Tartar of the steppe. You hear it in *Sadko* and *Scheherezade*. And in the music of Borodin: *In the Steepes of Central Asia*. To know this cruel story of the heart of Muscovy, I can think of no better books to recommend than three remarkable biographies by Stephen Graham: *Ivan the Terrible, Boris Gudunov*, and *Peter the Great*. These three fine books were not mugged up in the British Museum. Stephen Graham knew old Tsarist Russia like the back of his hand. These three biographies should be "required reading" for every Western diplomat, having to do, as he most certainly will for years to come, with Soviet Russia and her satellites. The life-story of these three brutal autocrats will help you to understand Josef Stalin: he is right in line. And so is current Russian history. In the last will and testament of Peter the Great (which is one of the most illuminating documents of Russian history, whether it is authentic or not) you will see that among the territories he thought it necessary that Russia should seize to ensure her own security he included Prague.

Stephen Graham tramped the Caucasus as old Wicksteed and I would now. That is the only way to get to know a country : to *experience* it at first hand, and not take the words of anyone, especially its official spokesmen, for what is going on. Wicksteed, in his little Dostoevsky-like cell, with his communal toilet, was far closer to the beating heart of Russia than any of the high-powered correspondents in the Grand Hotel could ever get. And we had some very impressive personages among us: gloomy intellectuals, with shaggy heads and frowning brows, writing profound tomes on the Soviet foreign policy, etc., taking the official hand-outs as they were fed to them. The conjuncture of a cheap university education in America, spread only skin-deep, with the sensational rise to importance of the foreign newspaper correspondent, meant that this woolly-haired intelligentsia—not one of whom had ever spent a night in the open country—were to be our interpreters of the truth from then on. I had to laugh to think that in nearly a year I had not heard one of them once mention the Oka: that here, less than 120 miles from Moscow, began the Asiatic who lurks behind all Kremlin policies. I take no credit for having heard of it, except that in the three years I spent in Tsarist Russia—from the winter of 1914-15 until after the Kerensky Revolution—I had reached the conclusion that if I intended to spend the rest of my life in Russia, make my career there as I hoped to do, I had better learn something about the country. In those three years I had to deal with the Russian War Department—enough to break any man's heart—and so it was partly in solace, partly curiosity, and ultimately an overwhelming fascination that made me read whatever Russian histories I could lay hands on, and all the great Russian novelists, again and again. The Time of the Tartar—where the two-headed Romanov eagle looks east—fascinated me most.

In the "white nights" of Petrograd, when things were going bad for me in the War Office, and I did not have enough money to go out to the Islands, get drunk, and hear the gipsies sing, I sat in my window overlooking St. Isaac's Cathedral—and stared east. Like the opium-eater's dream, I saw the towers and turquoise domes, the teeming bazaars, the camels plodding across the steppe—I vowed I would go there. In May of 1915—exquisite spring!—I was in the Crimea, and watched the water fall, drop by drop, from the pearl shells in the harem of Khan Tokhtmuish, of which Pushkin wrote his *Fountain of Tears*. I peered through shadowed lattice behind which this Tartar Khan kept his Circassian girls, and looked down at the pool in which they were allowed to bathe, with the tall Lombardy poplars whispering softly. . . . A Modammedan paradise. And then, on the top of the precipitous cliffs which overhang this flowered valley, I had visited Tchufut-Kalé, the Fortress of the Jews, the Karaïtes, who have no Talmud; whose walls, cut from natural stone, are twenty feet thick, and where the roads leading up across the soft sandstone had ruts worn by the wheels of centuries, so deep that they almost grounded the hubs of my own carriage. There in their valley of Jehosaphat I saw the Jews still putting roses on the tomb of the Khan's daughter, who, so it was said, had thrown herself from the rocks, in consequence of unrequited love (1437). That was the accepted historical version. But the Rabbi Gakham told me, as I ate his black bread and goat cheese, that the real story was that she eloped with a handsome young Jewish prince of Tchufut-Kalé; the infuriated Khan attacked the Jewish fortress to retrieve her; and when she saw her lover killed fighting on the walls, she threw herself from them. I liked that version better.

I was in love myself at that time (or thought I was) with the slip of young Russian girl who stood beside me in the Valley of Jehosaphat. Later, I decided that it must have been only the magic of that Crimean spring. I heard, after the war, that she had escaped from the Crimea with Baron Wrangel's forces, when his Cossacks, having failed to stem the Red Revolution, had to be evacuated. She had reached Constantinople, a Russian girl told me in New York. "But there"—this girl seemed very embarrassed—"we lost touch with her." Her flushed vagueness made me know that it was better not to want to learn what had happened to a beautiful young Russian girl who had been "lost touch with" in Constantinople. In 1925, when I was in that city, I looked for her, vaguely, among the girls, dressed in street clothes, who sat alone at tables with shaded lights, as you came into the *Rose Noir* at midnight. And in *Maxim's*, a gay little café-cabaret, run by an American negro, who had a Russian wife— a princess, he said! And, in quest, I even ate several meals at the *Turquoise*, where, it was said, every waitress was a Russian princess. But, of course, and as I have said, it is better not to know. . . . Spring in the Crimea; the minarets of Bakhtchi Sarai; the innocent little colt of a Russian girl, all legs, to whom I gave my precious V.P.K. camera in the Valley of Jehosaphat. Sentimental fool that I must have been. . . . No wonder those Tartar minarets along the Oka stirred uncomfortable memories.

I stayed out on deck one night to watch the dawn. It came about 2.30. Just a rose glow across the steppe. Then the ball of sun poured its red fire across it. Instantly, thousands of birds leapt into the sky to greet it. Larks spinning. Cliff swallows weaving patterns before our bows. We swung a bend, a sandy cliff, a wall of pine forest. Down below, on the foredeck, I saw a girl. We had the boat to ourselves, except for the man at the wheel. She was leaning, chin on her folded arms; and I saw her rise and hold up her hands to the sun as if in adoration. I went down to talk to her.

"I love it! Love it—love it—love it!" she cried, pointing at the steppe. "I love all Russia!"

I asked her where she was going. She didn't know, she said. She had been a typist in Leningrad, had saved her money. And now she was off! She was travelling third-class, to save money; going eastwards just as far as she could get. When her money ran out, wherever that was, she would get another job. When I asked her why she was so sure she could get one, her smile—she was a lovely little creature: blue eyes, pert chin, with one of those heart-shaped Slav faces—said, if translated freely: "Can a duck swim!" I saw her that night, laughing, up in the wheel-house with the First Officer. She gave me the impression that she would go a long way.

A precious lot she worried her pretty little head about the rights or wrongs of politics, the fact that she was not enjoying the delights of a parliamentary government: *Her* supreme love was *Russia*—just the land and the people. "Oh, how I love it!" she said to me with her engaging freshness as I resumed my place beside her next sunrise, watching the swallows play like dolphins before our bows: "If I could, I would roam around Russia all my life!" At that time I felt like replying: "So would I."

To me, this casual trip down the Oka—we seemed to stop everywhere, even to put a gang-plank on to a sandbar, to trade vodka for pigs—had a distinct Huckleberry Finn quality. The water would have been frozen had it not been in motion. But I had a swim at most of the long stops. Walking either up or down the river out of sight of the ship, stripping; a quick dive, then a lazy smoke while I lay on the sands and dried off in the sun. Old Wicker couldn't be tempted, not yet; but he usually came and sat beside me. One day the engineering student from Leningrad came with us, the man who was going to be a professor. He was fretted, indignant in fact, at the casual progress of our boat. The way we seemed just ambling down the Oka. He was afraid he would miss his boat to Rybinsk. He did.

"I know a little private pastry shop in Nijni," yawned old Wicker, "where we can get some real coffee. I got some there last September."

"Ah," said the Leningrad student, "nine months ago is not today."

"Trotsky's theory of the continuous revolution, eh?" said Wicksteed. "Everything has to change?"

"In nine months of Soviet Russia," snapped the student, "everything *does* change!"

The whistle blew, and we raced back to the ship.

We were approaching Nijni-Novgorod. Nijni on its green tableland was just a line of twinkling lights. The three domes of the Novy Sobor Alexander Nevsky on the almost submerged flats of the lower town rose up on our bows like a Venetian cathedral. In the pastel indistinctness of the lilac twilight they held enchantment. Red and green steamer lights speckled the busy waters down below; tugs with

· 52 ·

The start from Khassaut. Wickstead, with white beard, is next to the secretary of the Ispolkom and his wife

strings of yellow lights on their masts to show how many barges they had in tow. Oil coming up from Baku, limestone down the Oka, logs for Astrakhan. We would soon see the last of the lonely Oka, be back in a big city. The Russians were hanging over the bows for their first glimpse of the Volga. To them, it was like approaching a shrine. The life-stream down which their race had pushed eastward for ages.

"Is it the Volga?"

"No—not yet!"

We passed through a fleet of black fishing skiffs. I looked for the wooden bridge across the mouth of the Oka that is rebuilt every spring, saw that it was not up yet—and then found myself staring across a swirling silver flood.

"Volga! Volga!" cried the Russians, emotional as they are. But I felt the thing too. It was not the thought that I was looking on the largest river in Europe—the Volga is three times as long as the Rhine —it was just the sight of this mighty volume of water flowing past. Volga on its 2,300-mile journey to the sea. The superb indifference of the thing!

III

I STARTED to write an article about the Volga; I wrote three lines—and then I gave it up and decided to drown my futility in the company of a Russian girl whose diligence must be rewarded some time. Her repeated invitation, "You will go upstairs—yes?" meaning would I not go ashore—was as much a feature of this long river trip as the thousand miles of submerged forests on the left bank. But tonight she found me distrait.

"You see something—yes?"

"The Volga," I said, "it must be fifteen miles wide!"

"Yes?"

"Well, the last time I was here at this point it was only eighty yards."

"I do not understand—yes?"

"Look here," I begged; "have some sturgeon, have some horse-radish—do let me give you some more of this imitation French wine."

I filled her glass and went out on deck. Volga! How can I describe you—with what words could I convey the sleepy rustling of the aspens in the backwater of Spask? Or the shock of seeing the big steamer you wrecked there, her bones picked clean to the engine beds by your vulture ice. And what words can describe the utter desolation along your banks!

Or the depressing sight of that dead monastery we ran close to on the left bank. There it stood, forsaken and mournful; yet with all its fantastic towers and cupolas blazing with brilliant colours and gold. As reproachful a relic as I ever stared at (see photo facing page 17).

I had been down the Volga the year before, from Nijni to Astrakhan; and out to the Two Fathom Bank in the Caspian where that disastrous paddle-wheeler lay waiting for me; and, two hours after you think you have been at sea, you see a Kalmuck walking on water as Christ did on Galilee. The Kalmuck is shrimping. And your ship, of course, is in a channel. (But you won't see the Kalmucks any more.)

The Caspian rolls up in dirty waves across its miles of mud flats—pelicans troop with their gawky flight across the yellow evening sky; geese and long strings of ducks. Astrakhan, which is always spoken of as being on the Caspian, is no nearer that shallow saucer of water than Philadelphia is to the Atlantic, or London to the North Sea. As we steamed out of the Volga's muddy delta, 72 miles wide, we saw the fishing fleet coming in. Rough-built two-masters, black, with a sort of Asiatic standing lug. And as we passed them, fur-clad, slant-eyed men with high cheekbones stared up at us from loads of equally strange-looking fish. Kalmucks and sturgeon. Little skiffs bobbed out in the open shallow water; men in shaggy sheepskins leaned over their sterns, hauling gill-nets out of the brown sea, flapping glittering shavings of silver back into their black boats. . . .

The left bank, when the Volga is in flood, is nearly two thousand miles of submerged forests. From Nijni to Astrakhan you run down past a series of reaches and bays. The tips of birches and alders rustle and wave above the broad muddy flood. Buoys and range lights are sometimes fastened to trees. Down below Pokrovsk, in what was then the German Volga Republic, the spires of Lutheran churches and the tall, sharp-roofed grain elevators stand up like a silhouette of Danzig as you approach it from the sea. On the right bank, golden and painted cupolas of the Orthodox Church announce that a village lies ahead. A spray of wild caw-ing crows rises from the discredited Crosses, birds of ill omen; then they fly back and settle on the rigging of the crosses as you leave. The little Oka had been an ethnographic frontier. West of it were the Slavs; east began the country of the Finnish and Tartar tribes; the Tartars, Chuvash, Mordvins, Tcheremisses, Kalmucks, and Bashkirs.

We went ashore at Kazan so that Wicker could get a haircut. This ancient stronghold of the Golden Horde, so romantic from the river, with its white ramparts of the Kremlin and its pointed rose-coloured Tartar towers, was really, owing to the ineffectiveness of its modern Mongol inhabitants, not much more than a Slav city with a Tartar sauce. The fate of this branch of Genghis Khan's fierce horsemen is that they all ended up as waiters in the best restaurants of Slav Russia, where they still carry on. In the *droshky* which took us along the raised road into the city, we passed islands of log-rafts being floated in on the high water, so that they could be grounded right under the Kremlin's walls. We also passed a one-legged beggar, walking on two good legs, his wooden leg still attached and dragging behind him. "That's jolly," said Wicker, "he's walking to work!"

Wicker found a barber shop named *The Artist*. When he sat down Wicker-had a grey-and-white beard like a billygoat and a rough thatch of various-coloured hair on his head. Sort of a winter stubble. The barber took clippers and clipped his skull clean; then he took a shaving brush and lathered it until it looked like a pill. Then he shaved it. The beard he clipped to a sharp point. When Wicker arose he looked like a Mexican hairless dog.

"Nothing so refreshes me as to get my hair off," he said placidly. "You should try it."

I took one look at Wicksteed's skull—someone must have hit it with a hammer—and I said that I would keep my hair on. The city Russians invariably shave their hair in the spring and the sight of the craniums thus revealed is far from encouraging. But Wicker, God rest his gentle old soul, had out-Russianed the Russians even there. When we got back aboard the *Uritsky* we faced a rail lined with slant cheekbones and flowered skull-caps—we had a cargo of Tartars from Kazan.

Strange little Asiatic horsemen began to race the steamer on the islands lower down. They galloped their little horses along the shore. High, pointed hats, with the brims turned straight up. Red leather boots with the toes curled up. People shouted insults at them from our boat. All was so gay! Down there in that mass, almost mess, of mixed peoples, the accordions were going all day long. Gorky's *Lower Depths*—or like the East End of London—with all the rich, lovable, stinking humanity that prevailed. A sweating young man was dancing; banging down until his haunches hit his heels, then shooting one leg forward—"Whoop-whiskey-Popski!" Excruciating! And when they weren't dancing, and for some reason, perhaps exhaustion, the accordions were not going, all day long those lower depths wailed the Volga Boat Song. I never want to hear it again.

Yet that is one memory that I shall always carry with me from nearly five years of Russia. The deep, hopeful humanity of those river steamers—in those halcyon days of unimaginable freedom. (It was too good to be true, of course; yet no seer could have forseen its grim aftermath.) Day and night the steamer ploughs down to the

Caspian. . . . With the heavy-booted, bearded men getting off to go into the backwoods of the left bank, I was constantly reminded of Mark Twain's frontiersmen, as described in *Life on the Mississippi*.

We made no friends on this Volga boat. We, in the first-class, had passed out of the atmosphere of the friendly little paddle-wheeler on the Oka. That spell was broken. Two self-satisfied Comrades did try to get us into conversation; but as they knew so much more about the outside world than we did—they, who had never been more than five hundred miles away from Moscow—we did not feel equal to them. We lived in ourselves. In that world of imagination, slowly reading deep back into the days of old Russia, I lived again with Taras Bulba and the Cossacks of the Dnieper. I have never enjoyed that book so much: John Reed gave me my first copy, when he came in one day, with Boardman Robinson, to visit me where I was lying in the Post-Graduate Hospital in New York. That was 1916; and in that year I saw Nijinsky dance, in the Metropolitan Opera House, *Spectre de la Rose*. (John Reed's grave had been moved from beside Lenin's, when I went to look for it: he had been cast into everlasting damnation as a Trotskyist. "It would be better," said one of the few friendly Russians I met when I was back there in 1942—he was a young Foreign Office official in the Censor's Dept., soon to be killed by a land mine—"it would be better not to mention your friendship with John Reed.")

Wicksteed (and how that man could lose himself on a boat!) I would find lolling in an odd corner, feet up on another chair; pretending to read Shakespeare, but slyly putting honey in his beer. "*Mead*, y'know. Honey and beer. Favourite tipple of the old English monks. Try some?" He was in heaven.

We kept a "kitty." And as my paper was going to pay for the food, horses, etc., for all of this trip, not that it knew it, I suggested that Wicksteed let me be the banker. He accepted the office of Chancellor of the Exchequer. It was a sort of game that we played with each other; for—lo!—I would put ten roubles into the kitty; and—presto! —it would not be there. "But *how*?" I would cry. "At the last stop, all you bought was two cucumbers. Two cucumbers don't cost ten roubles. You had better check up." "Ah, yes. . . ." he would say absent-mindedly, moving one hand towards his pocket. But it never got there. Not to check up. Clearly, the right hand of Alexander Wicksteed did not know what it did. He had gone back into knee boots and *rubashka* again for this long Volga trip, and a black-visored white cap. He looked like a Commissar.

Our kitty on the Volga boat was transmuted into *mead*. He was no friend of the bottle, not by a long shot; but, as he often said, "the pleasure—or the oblivion—that one gets from alcohol is not altogether illegitimate. I must have some firm ground under my feet in the shifting sands of my disreputable life—one principle left—and that is: I never get up while there is any beer left."

In the days of the *boyars*, the rich merchants of the Volga—gigantic, over-stuffed men, like the immense brute, "with fingers big as cucumbers!" that poor Maslova was accused of poisoning in the Hotel Mauretania in Nijni-Novgorod, in Tolstoy's *Resurrection*—the Slav trading cities built along the banks of the Volga did have a certain amount of bourgeois impressiveness; and a fevered, small-town sensual life, lived to beyond the limits of sanity—such as Gorky pictured in *The Man Who Was Afraid*. But all that had been dead long ago. My delight in the broad vistas of the beautiful, shining river I did not want shattered by the squalor I knew I would meet ashore. So I refused even the most urgent invitations of the little Russian girl—"You will go upstairs, yes?"—by saying that I had been there before. Which I had.

This was her first trip. And she certainly wanted attention. Our beautiful Volga steamer was twin-screw; clean, comfortable, even luxurious, she would have been a credit to any country. Prowling about in her lower depths I met the chef, and he, moved by my appreciation of his work as an artist, led me to the side of his galley and showed me a live-tank in which were swimming hundreds of happy little sterlet. Holes bored in the ships side gave them a constant flow of fresh Volga water. One of the most delectable fish that swims, they look like miniature sturgeon, though they are seldom over a foot long. Their flesh is unbelievably delicate, and they are served with steaming boiled potatoes and sauce Hollandaise. When the chef gave us caviare for breakfast I wanted to stay on the ship to the Caspian.

"Caviare is so likesome!—yes?" said my steamer acquaintance. She was tragic. Tall and pale and awkward, her naïveté was painful. Definitely not of peasant stock, she had none of the arrogant self-assurance of the young Communist girls of that time. I judged her about twenty, which meant she was around eight years old when the Revolution broke out. Where that had struck her, from what background she came, I did not want to know. This Volga boat-trip was, all too obviously, one of life's great adventures for her. So I played the gallant and walked her around the deck as we would have on any trans-Atlantic liner.

The Volga was a constant story. The river traffic was fascinating. We passed immense barges being towed up, their decks awash, full of the "black gold," petroleum from Baku. They are hauled up the Volga by immense paddle-wheel tugs; a lovely sight, with the streaks of red lead from their shipyards blazing against a peacock blue river. For those people who lived in the few towns or villages on the left bank, landing barges were in some places anchored over a mile out in midstream, and passengers were ferried ashore from them in skiffs. We swung past log rafts floating down to the sea—with balconied houses built on them for their crews on the long journey. Lumber palaces, great overhanging structures like airplane carriers, made entirely of cut lumber—with a trellised walk between the two houses on the decks, fences to stop the babies from falling overboard, and red flags fluttering from their wooden belfries! In the Bow of Samara our ship steamed for sixty miles through a forest-clad elbow that might have been the banks of the Hudson, the only hills on the Volga. Below Saratov the right bank becomes bare cliff faces like the Grand Canyon of Colorado, serrated chalk and limestone—grey, with not a strip of verdure on their palisades. The Volga right bank here, the Hill Bank, is as hard as a bold seacoast; and here, in some sandy shores of the ravines, you will see little camps of sturgeon fishermen, with their nets spread out to dry, or long lines of bare hooks, black skiffs pulled up on the beach, pots hanging over their campfires. It was up this bend that the Volga boatmen, straining against the cruel tow-ropes, used to sing their sad song. Always, on the left, we passed the submerged forests, in reaches and bays, and long stretches where just the tips of the birches and alders swayed above the broad muddy flood. The wind-flecked Volga, galloping with white horses. . . . No man can give the feeling of this mighty river, except in song.

But here is one description that I take straight from my notebook. It is Stalingrad. I had plenty of time to write it; the train which we had expected to take us across the Don steppes ran, we found, only every other day. In fact, it had not run for thirteen days. Sitting in the dirty square, I wrote the following:

Stalingrad was the last and worst of the depressing Volga cities. . . . Perhaps the fact that we have lost a whole day might have accounted for our depression in this spot—but not for all of it.

It is difficult to define just the quality of dreariness of these Russian provincial towns. The old ones, like Old Novgorod, have inherited a romantic personality from the past, early churches and monasteries. But these Volga towns, marking the eastward expansion of the Slav, have, until very recent times, been nothing more than Cossack outposts. Stalingrad (old Tsaritzin), which was once held by Stenka Razin, the "Pirate of the Volga," was held by the rebel Pugatcheff (see Pushkin's *The Captain's Daughter*) in 1774; and for three months during the Red and White wars it was held by General Denikin, until the Reds drove him out in the bloody summer of 1919. It did not start to become a real town until Messrs. Vickers, the British armament people, built an artillery works here in 1914.

With dirty, dusty, cobbled streets, and a paper-cluttered square, Stalingrad plagues you with the awful desperation of a hot, sultry, summer afternoon, when you have nowhere to go. In Stalingrad there is nowhere to go. People just sit—and talk.

When Wicksteed suggested that I propose an alternative idea to his walking back to the railway station again to see if our tickets have been really bought for the midnight train, I could not think of anything better. There was a no more exciting adventure. But on the way up we encountered a funeral and attached ourselves to that. It was the burial of a child; and walking at the head of the procession was a little girl balancing the lid of a tawdry coffin on her head. The little silver-painted bound box was decked with flowers made of wood-shavings, dyed yellow and pink to imitate roses. It was carried by four other girls who had it slung in silk ribbons. We tramped with it to the outskirts of the town, where among unpainted board shacks some church bells were clanging crazily and a factory band was practising the *Budeney March*. And there we left it—with the priests chanting before the modern ikons of a red-brick church. Death, somehow, among such surroundings did not seem so sad.

The town itself was full of beggars, Russia's refuse. One man

Wickstead with the mountain police. Djhon-hote on the right, with Marusha. My Kolya on left

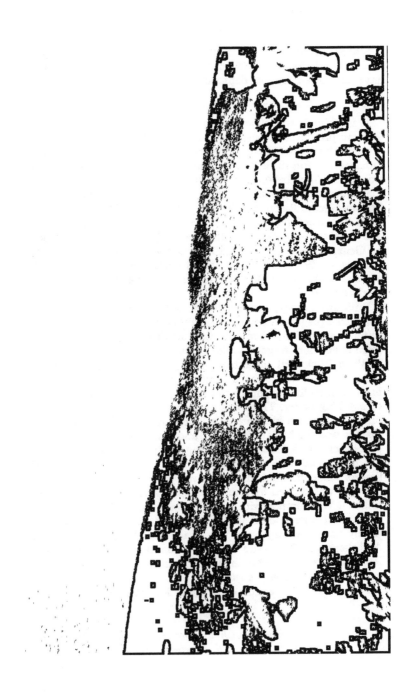

of a scientific trend of mind had fastened a spring on the bottom of his wooden leg, a shock-absorber. And here, I really believe, the squalor of Stalingrad is a solace—for the tattered beggar is not tortured by the sight of unobtainable delights.

Outside the Hotel Lux, communal, and the best establishment in the town, was a bread line that began somewhere behind it in the courtyard. Yet delicious fresh strawberries were being sold on the fruit stand before it for only 10 cents a pound. The elevator of the Hotel Lux has long ceased to work and has been turned into one of the weirdest abodes I have ever seen. Someone has made a house of it, boarding up the wire cage, with a glass window and green painted roof!

A placard on the wall of the communal dining-room showed a heroic worker standing on the top of the world, waving the red flag of revolution—and all the world's shackles dropping off. Most imposing. But the management of this proletarian eating place was so disturbed about his comrades that they made us pay for our food before we got it.

We went to the *Kacca* and paid the price of two cuts of small pig—which was both plentiful and excellent. Other placards on the wall, pointing the way to a new life, showed the ravages of venereal disease. Such cheerful frescoes!

The railway station seemed to be the most popular sleeping place in town. A crowd of *bez prizorney*, homeless ragamuffins and beggars, was sleeping along the outside walls until driven off by the police. And inside was the usual mass of wretched peasants stretched out on the stone floors. A young couple slept on a red quilt by the door, regardless of the shambles of bark-shod feet clumping past them. Inside the waiting-room men sprawled across the tables, sleeping on their folded arms.

One man sat on a bench, his wife kneeling, the upper half of her sleeping body resting across his knees. Their two children slept on the bench beside them, holding each other on.

The Russians always give the best places to their children. On another bench a flat-faced peasant woman had made up a bed for one child out of a little flowered quilt. A man and his wife and what was probably their full-grown son (I could see only his feet) had made up a real bed, with red quilt, and wooden suitcases for pillows, just beside the buffet. Some bewildered peasant girls, off,

· 61 ·

evidently, on some long pilgrimage, sat muffled in white sheepskin coats, from the folds of which their babies' heads stuck out. Some of them took out their breasts and fed them. Three Kalmuck men with two of their strange slant-eyed wives sat there inscrutably, hardly moving a muscle for five solid hours. Such absolute equanimity was disturbing. They were as complacent as their own Buddhas. I wandered but I was always drawn back to them.

Opposite the railway station was a garden of cool acacias. A band played inside it, and most of the population of Stalingrad seemed hanging enviously over its wire fence. When I tried to gain access to this haven I was stopped by a young Communist at its sacred gate. Was I a member of the Railway Transport Workers' Club? this impudent young girl demanded. No? well, I couldn't get in, then. And so I joined the other envious citizens and wondered about the ideals of a democracy that would turn a town park into such an exclusive club. Oh, freedom!

But back in the station I was cheered up by a beggar, a most original chap who really did give you something for your money. Not only did this tattered fellow play the mouth-organ, he also displayed tattooing of a Cross and a flight of doves. He showed a rosette worked round a spot where he had received a bullet in the Great War. He was the best artistic effort I had seen in town.

*   *   *

That was Stalingrad, 1929. Heroic Stalingrad.

IV

WE travelled "hard" across the Don Cossack country, sleeping on shelves, and awoke at six in the morning to see a moth-eaten camel plodding through the short wheat. It was pulling a man in a little low cart. The camel plodded along, with its supercilious stride, through fields of buttercups that it was crushing with its padded feet. The wheat rolled away to the blue horizon in wind-blown sunny waves. I looked out over sweeps of clover among the short grass, with larks spinning in the sky, and those queer little hooded, sparrow-like birds that one sees running everywhere along the sandy southern roads. These sweeping steppes, and the comfortable farmhouses that we came to, represented the finest free life on the land in country Russia.

The Cossacks are farmers, not peasants. Yeomen. (Or at least they were.) In the villages, founded around the *sotnia*—groups of a hundred horsemen—each white-washed, mud-walled house was set in a little enclosure of its own. Fences of wattle surrounded thatched houses and farm buildings, each with a cherry orchard and a pleasant yard shaded with acacia trees—a type of rural life unique in Russia. The dirt streets of the town were wide and long, planned regardless of space, which means nothing on the boundless steppes. The "centre," the town square, twice the size of any parade ground, was black with hundreds of horses and cattle. Knots of Cossack farmers and their families were collecting around a primitive merry-go-round just being put into action. The village of Marasovskaya was holding its weekly bazaar.

Then the steppes. . . . They rolled on, it seemed, for ever, in folds and grassy foothills. The blue bulk of clayey plateaux stood out like headlands at sea in the misty distance. They were cut and coloured by the beds of arid ravines. The dark wheat (all too little of it, it seemed) made vivid contrast with the grey steppe grass, which, at this early hour, still glistening with dew and gave the bare foothills the

· 63 ·

appearance of being covered with hoar frost. Horsemen stood out distinctly ten miles away. And over all this curved the great bowl of blue sky, in which white clouds seemed to float motionless. We went like this for 400 miles. Vast, illimitable, boundless space—the country of the Cossacks.

I am trying to keep politics out of this book as much as possible. But in September of 1929 I saw this Cossack life smashed. With Paul Scheffer, of the *Berliner Tageblatt*, I managed to get down there at that time and write the first eye-witness stories of the forced collectivisation of the farms, when this land of the Cossacks was being taken away from them. Even now, in the spring, the intelligent Cossacks knew that the long arm of Moscow was reaching out to take their free life away from them. And our railway carriage was full of a bitter resentment. People were silent, did not talk even to each other. When we reached the old capital of the Don Cossacks, Novotcherkassk, proud on its hill, where General Kaledin, *atman* of the Cossacks, shot himself when he was defeated by the Bolsheviks in 1918, I thought that the huge Red Artillery camp park outside of the town was not without significance. The Whites had recaptured this town and held it till 1920, as capital of an independent Don. The Kuban Cossacks of the Caucasus made trouble for Moscow as late as 1935. And will again, I hope, one day.

Novotcherkassk was a picturesque little capital, golden crowned with mighty churches, lying beside the Axai river, which, at this time of the year, in flood, was so wide in many places that I could not see its far bank; another illusion adding to the sense of vast space and the freedom of Cossack life. I thought of how, on March 12th, 1917, I stood in the snowy streets of Petrograd and saw the Don Cossacks laughing as they tried to make order among the growing mob of sullen people. They were not using their swords or whips! It was *then* that I knew that the Revolution, which we had all been expecting, had come. And on the night of November 7th, 1928, at a dinner given by the Soviet Foreign Office to celebrate the eleventh anniversary of the "October" Revolution (the Russian calendar is thirteen days behind ours), I danced with the beautiful young wife of General Budenny, whose Cossacks had captured this last Cossack stronghold in 1920. Cossack against Cossack. It was something to muse over as our train pulled us into the sunset—away from Novotcherkassk.

At Rostov-on-Don, capital of the Northern Caucasus, we were

already in the melting-pot of those mountain tribesmen. There were marked differences in all the people around us now. One group in particular held our attention, because theirs was the very country we were headed for. They were Turco-Tartars; cat-footed men, with shaved heads, wasp-waisted *tcherkasska*, with silver-tipped cartridge stalls across their breasts and silvered daggers in their belts. They bowed, with great ceremony, as they passed the vodka to each other (and they were Mohammedans!), touching each other's hands as they took the decanter in their token of thanks.

If ever west does meet east we were sitting on that spot. The station floor was strewn with faces and figures as different from each other as the colours on any map. They were unalike from head to feet. The Russian colonists going down into the wheat lands of the Kuban (to replace the Kuban Cossacks who had fought and fled with the Whites, or been executed or expropriated) wore heavy leather boots with great splay soles. The Caucasians wore soft black leather, with no soles at all—boots as thin as a glove—while their slender black beards were sharp-pointed in contrast to the Slavs' bushy growth. The eyes of the Caucasians were slanted and dark: the Russians' were round and blue.

The Russian women wore white kerchiefs tied under their chins, while the tails of their blouses stood out all around. And their faces were broad and flat. The Caucasian girls wore turbaned scarfs of vivid colours swathed around their oval heads; and their printed frocks were gay with flowers, high-waisted and slim. Under the frock, you saw, most of them were wearing trousers. And among these were hook-nosed Mountain Jews, speaking Tat, and flabby-faced Persians in cylindrical hats.

And painfully present in all this, expressed in the contrast of both face and figure, was the overwhelming determination of the Slav, the heavy-booted Great Russian, to take the lands of other people. But at that time, of course, all this was being done under the banners of the Revolution: the road to the New Life. These bovine Slav peasants, packing the railway station, were being set down like cattle—to graze on new fields. Most of them, if given a map, could not have told you where they were.

We caught the midnight train out, travelling "longitudinal." This is an experience which cannot be described. For a longitudinal is one of these shelves *inside* the aisle, made by turning up the seat flaps;

which seem to have been constructed for a man five feet high and ten inches wide. If you do not fit in with these dimensions you will not fit a longitudinal. Folded up like a foot ruler (Wicker was a comfortably smaller man than me) I clung to my perch all night. It was no wonder that I saw this dawn rise. We changed into a little mountain train at Mineral Water, which for the first hour went through the last of the Don Cossack lands; then we crossed a muddy swirling river, and began to pass among the scattered villages of the Cossacks of the Kuban. Vast monotonous rising plains; and then—a white cone began to appear in the sky.

It was Mount Elbruz, an extinct volcano, seen from sixty miles away. (When we were on horseback in the lower ranges of the Caucasus we did not see it again for weeks). Three thousand feet higher than Mt. Blanc, it thrust up in unbroken sweeps of white snow behind the skyline of the steppes, terrible in its majesty. Its name means White Breasts. And although, even from right under it, it looks like a sharp-pointed cone, there is a mile between its two peaks, its two nipples.

That noon we reached Kislovodsk. Our jumping-off place into the frosty Caucasus.

V

KISLOVODSK was a town of shimmering poplars swaying in the bright sun, green hills, and a sparkling river. A cool wind from the mountains brought the exciting smell of spring snow. In the old days, from around 1840 to 1870, this little spa had been the fashionable watering place for the Tsarist officers of the Army of the Caucasus and their pretty women. A place of rendezvous, lovers' trysts, of picnics on horseback into the wild ravines of the mountains, of arched eyebrows plucked by pretty fingers; the mazurka, gold epaulets—and duels. It was here that Lermontov had Petchorin, that sardonic *Hero of Our Times*, play with the heart of the trusting Princess, and kill his brother officer Grouchnitzky in the duel—making that luckless fool take the edge of the cliff, as he did himself, so that if either one of them was hit, and only staggered, he would be dashed to death on the rocks down below—precisely the same way that the great poet himself was killed in a duel with a brother dragoon officer at Pyatigorsk, 1841, only a few miles below Kislovodsk, and only a year or so after that little classic *A Hero of Our Times* had made Lermontov the idol of literary Russia. At Kislovodsk many a good man had been "drowned in love."

Now all that was over. Romance was gone, beauty was dead. And Wicksteed and I, wandering around in our search for horses, felt as alien in that hostile existence as if we had been invaders from another planet. The faces of even the old buildings had changed—and refused us admission. The Grand Hotel, the Park, etc., these had now become the Red Stone, Red October, the Karl Marx Sanatorium, even the Dzerjensky (late head of the dreaded Cheka)—all reserved for responsible Communist Party workers—and no arched eyebrows plucked by pretty fingers or any bourgeois nonsense about being drowned in love for the factory lads and lassies (if such there were among that lot) who now inhabited them. Love had been put on a "natural" basis; like an animal going on heat. It was about as unappetising and vexatious an atmosphere as I ever want to breathe. Even old Wicksteed, indefatigable champion of the proletariat, had to mutter as we stared at the odiously arrogant, happy, and hostile faces, all staring at us, in the Narzan Gallery.

"This is a *beastly* place! Already ruined by the tourists! I would not want to spend a night here, even if we *could* stay!"

I had to smile: that he should call his beloved *Bolsheviki* "tourists!" But do not think for a second that, at that time, I felt that way towards all Communists. Far from it. In roving about Russia I had met Communist after Communist whose devoted self-sacrifice and zeal had aroused my envy. They were afire with energy and belief in the new life. The West itself was rather short of inspiring beliefs at that time: some Cause to serve which was bigger than oneself. And I think that this—this spectacle of finding people who really believed in their faith, like the ancient Christians—was where most of the fellow-travellers were made. But this lot, these fat-armed grinning men and women, so slyly cocksure and pleased with themselves, who had got themselves into the rest homes of Kislovodsk—these were not "workers"; they were the exploiters, the speech-makers, the spivs of the Revolution—it seemed written on their foreheads. These were the new privileged class. I loathed them.

These springs of sparkling Narzan at Kislovodsk are enough to break a man's heart. It is a very highly prized mineral water, something like Apollinaris, which pours out here at the rate of about half a million gallons every day. A White Russian in Paris would give his last franc for a bottle of it. This had been a favourite drink of the wild mountain tribesmen long before a Russian ever stepped foot in the Caucasus. "The drink of heroes!" they called it. And they had *bathed* in it for centuries. Some, it must have been, for the sheer delight of wallowing in such exciting stuff (it is the most amazing feeling!); but most because of the ancient, and still held, belief in their magic medicinal qualities. For example, the mountaineers (and not only the mountaineers!) firmly believe that bathing in Narzan is a great way to allay the pains of venereal disease. Some optimists think that, if you carry on long enough, Narzan baths are even a cure for it. So it was that when Alexander Wicksteed was wallowing in one of these cosy little pools up in the wild mountains a few weeks later, with two very hairy and talkative Karachaites, and he asked them why they came and, as they said, lay in this particular pool for

Caucasian horsemen

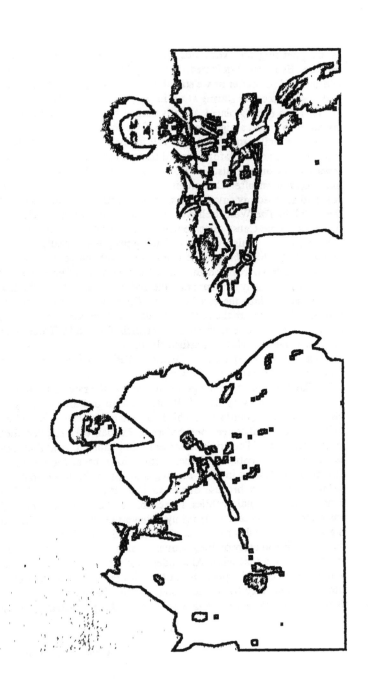

at least an hour every day, he received the grinning reply: V.D.—
and was shown that they were both suffering from a bad case of it.

"Great God!" he cried to me afterwards· "I won't feel safe for
weeks!" I told him that he could be like the little dog and say that
he got it from a lamp post.

Old would-be-Russian Wicksteed did not mind so much—and it
was this continual conflict in our opinions which gave this trip such
unique spice—but I was furious that after our long, lazy, and hopeful
trip across Russia, we should arrive at Kislovodsk, and find that we
had come right back to the old boring Moscow atmosphere again: all
the suspicions, the politically indoctrined hates. I do not wish to
appear wise after the event. My personal feelings, in reporting what
was going on in the land of the Soviets, at that time, were: first, it
was a pity that so many good, kind-hearted, and even harmless
people should have been murdered to make this proletarian paradise,
if it ever was to be a paradise; next, after faithfully reporting all the
material achievements that the Bolsheviks had set themselves to
accomplish, I would search with eagerness for every improvement I
could honestly report that the Communists had made in the art of
living, if I could find any. As the latter score still stood at zero, and
was even going below—except for show pieces—it can be understood
why the faces in the Narzan gallery struck me as being odiously
happy: they were mutton. Sheep. And their ignorance about the
outside world was invincible. The clear streams, the snowy mountains,
the deep pine and fresh beech forest, all the ever new and radiant
beauty of nature—these idiots, with their materialistic conception
of life, would deny anything but utilitarian values: what they could
get out of them. Staring at them, I thought that while the mountains
themselves, the sheer rocks, might defy them, the mountaineers
could not: this spring of 1929 was probably the last when one could
ride up among the tribesmen in the higher Caucasus and still be
among free men. . . .

I think old Wicksteed's costume might have had a little to do with
our inability to get horses, and the immediate stares of either fear
or suspicion that were invoked by our appearance. On the way up
on the train from Mineral Water he frenziedly unpacked one of his
rucksacks—and unearthed (for that is the appropriate word) his
beloved Ossetine hat. This was a flapping white mushroom affair,
which, with his shorts, bare knees, and white beard, made him look

something akin to both a perambulating toad-stool and a Prophet. Why did a man like that want a horse? Ah !—And people shied from him like horses. Even the G.P.U. at the railway station (usually so helpful) seemed worried by him.

In the park was a kiosk, inside which sat a Circassian in all the glory of his belted *tcherkasska*, cartridge-covered breasts and silver-handled dagger. He was an exhibit, a hawk they had brought down from the upper mountains, to impress the Comrades with the picturesque wildness of their Bolshevik Baden Baden. He was selling postcards, and not averse to talk. And while he talked to us of bandits, showing us where they had shot him through the stomach and chest—he had killed them both for their impudence—he warmed and became more confidential over the snows and the trails of the Karachaite country This was where I broached horses. . . . Yes, it would be better, he said, leaning forward not to be overheard, if we got our horses "inside." Take a *lineaka*, a mountain cart, over the lower ranges to Khassaut. The Mohammedans in there were great horse traders. There was an old Kuban Cossack in Kislovodsk who had a *lineaka*. He could usually be found, sleeping off a drunk, with his back against the wall of the old Tartar mosque down in the bazaar. . . .

So it was not by intention that we set out to cross the lower ranges of the Caucasus in the night. We found our Uncle Eroshka; a black-bloomered old hedgehog, with a shaven grey pate. "Certainly!" he said. "Me and my little horses can take you to the moon, if you want to go there!" And he won my heart by shouting when we told him we had left our rucksacks, etc., with the G.P.U. at the railway station: "Aie! *Svallich!* those sons-of-bitches!" He also called me "Dear one!" when I stopped the *lineaka*, and hurriedly got off, a few miles outside the town, suggesting that we have one for the road. He must have had springs in his fat hams, that old rogue; for the *lineaka* hadn't any! "Dear one—it's *full!*" he cried, as he hefted the huge porcelain flask of vodka. But it was a lot emptier when he handed it back to us. After that I walked. . . . It was a gloomy sunset, but he hoped for a moon. This, as luck had it, began to look down through its torn blanket of clouds just when we needed it most. When it caught us picking our way along the rocky face of a cliff where the crags stood out sharp above a deep valley filled with mist, and we looked down to see the fork where two silver rivers joined, and lay waiting for us under the moon. . . . It was enchantment: Wicksteed and I blessed the delays that had led us to such a spot at just such a time. We paused here, and had another one for the road, while old Uncle Eroshka lashed the wheels of his little *lineaka* with chains, so that they would not revolve, and he could slide his cart like a sledge down the steep rocky ledge that led down into the valley. "Steady!— my darlings!" he kept warning his two remarkable little horses. "Be quiet!"

The road leading into the upper reaches from Kislovodsk had given no indication whatever of this country. It climbed instead into an amazing upland that was smooth as a lawn. Fold after fold of vivid green hills with not a stone or bush on them. Here and there, only, a ledge of limestone broke through; and a peek over the grassy edge into the grey gorge of the river below assured us that we were actually in the Caucasus. We kept climbing that way into the upper reaches of the sunset. At about 5,000 feet, with Kislovodsk lost behind us among the tablelands of its windless valley, we might have been in an uninhabited world. We had been climbing for hours without even seeing one sheep. One or two Caucasian horsemen had passed us, magnificent in their broad-shouldered black *burkas*, made from woolly felt almost a quarter of an inch thick, wearing their silvered daggers. Finally, I saw what seemed to be a haycock on fire; but it had a low wall of mountain stones around its bottom; and a man sitting in a smoky aperture showed it to be a house. Our first Karachaite.

"*He* lives poorly!" sniffed our Uncle Eroshka, still feeling his ancient Cossack superiority over mountain tribesmen. "Life is hard here."

That was true. And this was the first of those stone igloos, called *koshes*, in a few of which we were to sleep ourselves later on. Just flat stones piled on top of each other, without moss or plaster, a sod roof, no chimney, and the smoke finding its way out as best it could. Yet when a good hailstorm was raging we found them delightfully comfortable. The downs began to give way to ridges, and on the top of one of these Wicker and I made the old Cossack stop so that we could get out our sweaters and heavy jackets. As night descended the wind seemed to increase. We were freezing. And it was only then that the cheery old rascal saw fit to mention that there had been a snowstorm the day before in these ranges. He seemed particularly anxious to get on, and battened down our bed-rolls and rucksacks with half-hitches over everything. Otherwise everything would have slid off, as the *lineaka* has a flat body with no sides, is light, built like a spider, to give the horses the minimum to pull; and, springless as it is, it bounces from rock to rock.

"Hurry!" he urged—and said that the road was very bad ahead. But we continued to ascend more smooth hills, their upper levels carpeted with alpine flowers that shone like stars under the moon. It was as if the heavens had been upturned. We went across waving slopes carpeted with little swaying flowers that looked like butter-cups in the daylight. Higher and higher. . . . The mountains below us began to drop off sharply, lost in the mist; we saw the outline of new ranges, the white snow in their ravines. . . . New countries. Over the ridges of the lower mountains to our right lay the country of the Kabarda-Balkarians, people of Turco-Tartar and pure Arabian blood. Their capital had once been the commercial centre for Byzantium. It was these sophisticated, softened, trading people who had refused to join the great Shamil, in his last wild guerilla campaign against the Tsarist Russians, and thereby forced his surrender, and the end of the 160 years' Caucasian war between Cross and Crescent. Flanking us lay the Ossetes, who, lying across the centre of the main chain, sold the key of the Caucasus to the Russians—the Mamison Pass. Only the East and the West of the Caucasus fought the glittering Russian bayonets. Southwards, over the snows of the main chain, lay Suanetia: not visited by any traveller until 1854, says Dr. Abich, the German ethnologist, who got in there himself at that time. Beyond, farther to the east, stretched the ancient Kingdom of Georgia, where they were wearing the purple when the Britons were still painting themselves blue with woad; ancient Iberia, whose Mountain Jews firmly believe they are the descendants of Dan, one of the Lost Tribes of Israel. And as soon as we topped the next ridge that rose against the stars ahead of us, we ourselves would be in Karachay—"Up to 1820 the fierce tribes of the Karatshai (Kara-chaites) prevented any attempt to penetrate their fastnesses," says Douglas Freshfield. But the Greeks knew them. Pliny writes of them coming over the Klukhor Pass with climbing-irons (*crampons*, still used in the Caucasus) and toboggans—sliding down past the glaciers to the ancient city of Dioskurias, near the present city of Sukhuum on the Black Sea. That strikes a sportive note in their character which on occasions old Wicksteed and I found that they did indeed possess! "Karachay! Karachay!" the old chap exhulted. "We are now in the land of 'water wet, grass green, and mountains steep!'" He was right about the last part of it.

It was while we were paused here, our souls filled with delight, that we heard soft padding behind us. Two superb Karachaites came up from behind on their glistening black stallions. In a soft drawl they asked us whence, whither—why? Our answers could have been calculated to surprise them: but they gave no sign of it. They lit cigarettes, they wrapped their white hoods over their fur caps, and dropped over the edge. . . .

Here, the Cossack told us, we had better walk in the rear of the *lineaka*, away from the horses. And walk about twenty paces apart— so that we would keep out of each other's shadows, and thus not stumble and fall off the cliffs. He walked at their heads, talking to them affectionately as they frequently backed up against the sliding cart. "Whoa! my darlings—take it easy. . . ." Just before we dropped over, with the moon picking out the wild flowers, I looked across the ridges of mountains and had a last stare at Mt. Elbruz . . . which I didn't see again for three weeks.

When these two little wire-muscled horses had been standing still in Kislovodsk, they looked like weary nags. When they were moving, dragging the cart by sheer guts up the bouldered mountain roads, or sliding down—with the rear wheels locked by chains—they put up such an exhibition of courage and cool-headedness that I positively loved them.

The slide down seemed interminable. The hours crawled. It got colder and colder. Finally things became desperate. I could no longer light a cigarette. My fingers were too numb. From Kislovodsk to Khassaut was twenty-four miles, the tame Circassian in the kiosk had told us. I felt that we had more than covered it. And I demanded if there ever was such a place as Khassaut.

"Here it is," said the Cossack.

He got off and rolled back a strange gate that had a wagon-wheel on its latch-end. The moon had gone under by now, and in the gloom I caught the white bullet of a minaret. I made out the squat shape of a domed mosque underneath. There were, of course, no lights in the village. We drove past some sleeping thatched huts. Then we stopped before a building which the Cossack said was the school. Here, said

· 73 ·

the Cossack of the Kuban, Khassaut would put us up for the night. But not so the schoolmaster!

"But these are strangers!" bellowed the furious Cossack after a terrific hammering on the schoolmaster's boarded window. "These are your guests!"

A muffled voice from within told us to go away and come back in the daylight.

We then tried the Ispolkom, the village council chamber, where our reception was exactly the opposite. As soon as he got it into his sleepy head that there were foreigners outside, the secretary of the Ispolkom, who slept in one of its two rooms, unbolted the door. He was, noble fellow, suffering from toothache, with the rabbit's ears of a bandaged poultice projecting upward from his head. But he led us into his own bedroom, where his wife eyed us from among her bed of quilts spread out on the board floor. Beside her lay a rifle and a leather bandolier (see photo facing p. 48). The secretary told us to spread out our beds beside theirs. When we told them that we did not wish to intrude upon their privacy (it was not altogether from modesty: the double windows of that room had been shut all winter) he led us into the town council chamber. Here he brought some birch logs and started the iron stove. He gave us a pail of sparkling water, a glass of butter—and his only lamp. Uncle Eroshka began to carry our stuff in.

"Tell me," I asked the old Cossack, interested by the sight of the rifle lying beside the secretary's wife on the floor, and that squeaky voice of the schoolmaster, which had so obviously been full of fright. "Why wouldn't the schoolmaster let us in?"

"Ha-Ha!" The Cossack gave a great guffaw and slapped his baggy breeches. "He was *frightened*! You see, these people here—these ignorant Karachaites—they *shot* the schoolmaster before him."

VI

IT was a nice thought to go to bed on. But what made it so especially interesting to me was the fact that I had seen the counterpart of this very murder enacted in the incomparable little Art Theatre. I think it was in *The Armoured Train*, or it may have been in *The Days of the Turbins*—those two really stirring plays that were produced by the Revolution. At any rate, the audience sees a house in a backward peasant village, and the shadow of a man cast on the pulled-down blind of a lighted window; the shadow of a self-sacrificing young Communist who has come to "enlighten" the village. It is night: utterly silent. Oh, silent night, ominous night . . . the genius of Stanislavsky knew how to put that across. The young Communist is reading; and all this acting is done so superbly that you even feel his weariness, and his *danger*, as he turns over page upon page by the lighted window—until you hear the shot! The shadow slides forward across the table. . . .

Despite the cold, which crept along the floor and made my spine feel like ice, and showed me well in advance how woefully inadequately our mountain kit had been selected (I bought a half-inch thick Karachaite felt rug the first thing I did the next morning), the sleep that old Wicksteed and I had on the hard floor of the council chamber was the first real night's rest that we had enjoyed for several days. We didn't have much, however: shortly before dawn I was awakened by a noise at our window—and there appeared the hedge-hog head of our Cossack driver. He was standing on his flat cart, as the Ispolkom was built on a slope, with his two little wire-muscled nags, their heads down, waiting patiently. He had come to say good-bye. "Good-bye, dear one," he croaked, when I had reluctantly got out of my flea-bag to take his outstretched paw. "Be happy in the mountains!" I could have done without such affection, having paid him off and given him a good tip only a couple of hours back. But perhaps the old fellow really liked us. Why not? I told him to wait, and went back to fetch the vodka flask, which I handed to him. "Drink it all," I said. "All!"

"*All?*" he gasped, hardly able to believe his ears—"Word of God!" He swigged down about a pint without drawing breath. It would have knocked out an ordinary man. Looking up the bronze valley, I saw the sun blazing like fire on the crest of the far bluish mountains. It was no priggish resolution that prompted me to ask him to drink all that was left of our precious vodka (Wicker nearly cried when he found out what had happened); it was just that in that freshness of the morning, and the sight of those beautiful mountains blazing in the sun, I wanted to start this ride fresh. I didn't want any false enthusiasms to blur my senses. "Be happy!" I said to old Uncle Eroshka, which is the customary form of one Russian saying farewell or speeding another Russian off on a journey. "Happy? Well, maybe. . . . May the devil take me!" he laughed hoarsely. "Now *I'm* off for home!" I only hope that his two little nags got him there.

Wicker had slept through all of this; a sweet, self-exultant smile on all that appeared of his white-bearded face. He slept with his old Ossete hat on. He was cosy as a tick in his home-made little bed-roll and kapok mattress. I knew by now the mysterious contents of his two battered rucksacks, so I got out the little spirit lamp and made myself some coffee. Time was ours now, and we could do what we liked with it. Then, looking up, I saw a Mongolian face examining me from the doorway. It vanished, and came back in a few seconds with a whole horde of Mongolians. All in fur hats. "What do you want?" I asked. But none of the faces, some of them so slant-eyed that they might have been Chinese, seemed to know what to answer. Small, ugly, swarthy, blue-jowelled, and beady-eyed, they stared at me silently. I poked Wicker. "Wake up," I said to him. "We've got company."

"Wha—?" He rolled over and stared at them. "Interesting-looking lot, aren't they," he said to me over his shoulder. "What would you have done? . . . er . . . ahem," he said, sitting up. "Friend of mine, he was riding with some of these chaps in a railway train, when one of them bet the others that he could pluck a live fowl; which he then proceeded to do to the enjoyment of all. . . ."

I told him to shut up and drink his coffee, and in the meantime find out what these people wanted. "It appears," he said profoundly, after a few words with a tall red-bearded individual, who now stood

A kosh in the Caucasus

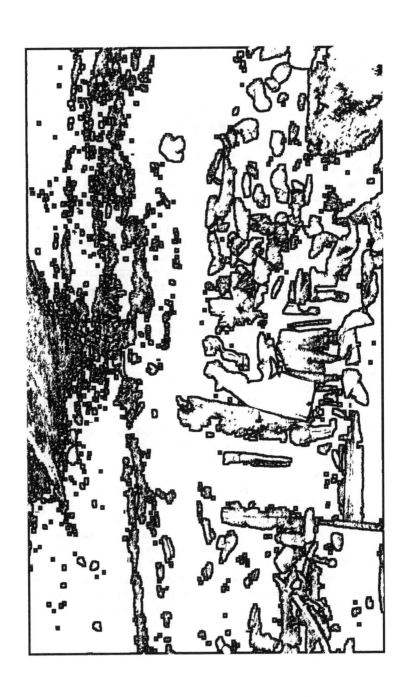

at the back of the little Tartars, "that they want to hold a meeting." He looked at his wrist-watch. "Six o'clock. Rather early—for a meeting—don't you think?"

"Meeting be damned," I said to him. Then to the tall man I said in Russian: "Tell these people to go."

He tried to. But an awful row broke out. This brought the little secretary of the Ispolkom, on the run. He sailed into them. What he said to them was in Karachaite, but we had a fair idea of what it was: he was upbraiding them for their bad manners. Then they all sailed into him. Their protestations were so furious that it almost looked as if knives would be drawn. Then the big fellow, the tall chap with the red beard, burst through them all with an outward sweep of his two arms, like a swimmer taking a breast stroke. "Listen!" he said to the little pale-faced secretary in good Russian. "These two strangers can sleep here all morning, all day if they want to: only—why can't we *look*?"

And that was all, it turned out, that the row had been about. They had come there to watch us get dressed. As Wicker and I had turned in with nearly all our clothes on, taking off only our shoes and jackets, that did not give them much of a treat. The embarrassed Tartars moved off.

With that courtesy that is always to be found among primitive people unspoiled by tourists, the secretary of the Ispolkom and his wife had put their room in order for our breakfast. His wife was our hand-maiden, dipping a tin mug into the bucket of sparkling Narzan—fetched from a spring across the river—and pouring it over my head and hands as I washed. An ancient custom, and the flesh-tingling Narzan made me wish I could have a full bath in it there and then. The tall man with the red beard, who seemed to have made himself master of ceremonies by now, came to the doorway and stood there, terribly interested in what I was doing with my tooth-brush. And I, seeing his even white teeth when he smiled, wondered how he kept his so clean. A mutual curiosity. I had yet to learn the use of the little stick, bashed into a fuzz at both ends, with which these shaggy mountaineers keep their teeth clean as polished ivory. And I did not know then, of course, that this—this very man, with his long silvered dagger and glove-soft leather boots—that this gallant d'Artagnan, with the swagger of a fur hat cocked to one side, would be the first man who, despite some local opposition, would supply our first pair of horses, and come with us into the upper Caucasus. He was a pure-blooded Circassian, and his name was Djhon-hote. No gayer companion, if a bit unpredictable, ever toasted himself before a camp fire.

There was a sort of an odour of honest simplicity about Djhon-hote, sometimes very strong: he asked no more than to be allowed to live with horses, love them, and have a free life with them. He was the very spirit of the wild Caucasus. He looked on every Russian as a natural enemy of this free life in the mountains; which, of course, was precisely what they were.

A day or two later, when we were camped in the mountains, I caught him using my toothbrush. And as I took it away from him—telling him the old joke, that there are three things a man never loans another man: his razor, his toothbrush, or his wife—I knew from his laughter that he was going to use something other of mine the moment he got the chance.

"Ah, yes," groaned the secretary's wife, "they hold meetings all day long! Meetings, meetings, meetings—and it is always about horses!"

That was good news to us. Horse breeding and selling, it seemed, was the life of the Khassaut Karachaites. A horse auction began outside while we were at breakfast. This was being held around a three-forked tree trunk stuck up outside the small council chamber. We were to see these same symbolic tree trunks all along the slope of the North Caucasus. The same strange three-forked hitching post that we were to see outside *koshes*, and even in the capital of the Karachaites. It was when you reached that tree trunk that you dismounted, and waited for the formality to be completed before you were invited to be the guest of either kosh or village. It was also the auction block.

With the men of the village lounging around, leaning against rocks and walls in the warm sun, a bearded auctioneer in belted Caucasian *tcherkasska* and soleless boots, with the usual dagger in his belt, called out the bids as he rolled a cigarette. He did so casually, urging no one to buy, and he seemed to knock off when he thought the price about right. At any rate, with these keen judges of horseflesh—they are all but born on a horse—there was not much chance of anyone being reckless.

Another Tartar, for my amusement, shinned up the three-forked tree trunk and sat there. A childish bit of fun for a man with a two-foot fluted dagger in his belt. If you can—picture these horsemen in a little mountain village of thatched stone houses, with a minaret like a stick of chalk standing up against the blues and greys of some nearby limestone crags, selling and buying horses, galloping down the main mud road after wandering cattle, reaching down at full gallop to pick from the ground one of their sheepskin hats which they had thrown there in mere bravado, rounding up the grey cattle, smoking, gossiping, lying flat on their faces in the warm sun—you have a perfect picture of Khassaut on a Sunday morning. Friday is the Mohammedan day of rest.

And like all good Mohammedans they were letting the women do all the hard work. Outside one stone hut beside us the women were softening some sheepskins. They were kneading them between wooden pincers. One woman pumped up and down on a long handle while a girl turned the skin between the notched wooden teeth until it turned soft as chamois. Most of the Karachaites were indeed wearing *shubas*, which is a Russian peasant coat made of sheepskins with the woollen side in. Most of them stink worse than a decomposing sheep; and one I brought home in 1917, and gave to a Welshman who helped me get in the Royal Flying Corps, was so awful that his fond mother said that he could choose between "that dreadful coat" and a room in the house. As he couldn't find anyone to give it to, I think he finally buried the coat.

Outside another stone and plaster house, on whose sod roof was already growing a good crop of grass, an old crone was weaving on a handloom. Another hag sat beside her spinning thread from a plummet-like spindle, which she set whirling with a sharp rub against her old leg. The Fates of the Karachaites—of what battles with the Cossacks of the Line could these old women tell!

Women were working in the meagre potato fields, the only village crop. Others walked gracefully across the single log which bridged the Khassaut river and returned swaying under yoke and pails of spring water. The mosque, which no woman dared enter, was completely carpeted with small rugs. Vivid in colouring and almost cubist in design; the thick felt rug of the Karachaites, made of natural dyes: black, white, orange. None of your graceful, intricate Persian patterns here. And as I lay there in the warm sun, as lazy as any Karachaite himself, I watched the little sons, dressed in little

· 79 ·

tcherkasskas, with miniature dagger in belt—just like father's—ride beautiful black stallions down to water. And even the tiniest girls were at work—just like mother. Picturesque, but these Asiatic women were still considered the drudges, despite the female emancipation proclaimed outside the mountains by the Soviets. We were "inside" now: on the far side of the wall of mountain down which we had slid the previous night lay advancing Communist Russia. From now on, in the *koshes* and in the native *aouls*, small mountain villages clinging like birds' nests to the ledges, we would be in the country of the Old Man of the Tribe, the patriarchal rule, with all its good and bad customs.

A bit of advancing Moscow had, however, got over this wall. This was an ex-Red Army soldier. Usually, when I was in a country village, I began by looking at the *feet* of the people who always made a circle around me. If I saw one with good quality leather boots, kept in good condition, I could be almost certain that he had been in the Red Army. I could also be almost certain that he had been sent back, as an example or instructor, to his own village. Usually they were very helpful; and in those eager and faith-inspired days they would go to any length to show the countryside to me, and explain what stage the village had reached, both its progress and its backwardness. But in Khassaut I was followed about by one surly fellow (see man on extreme right in photo facing page 48) who at once came up to every person that I had had a few words with, and, seemingly, put him or her to a severe questioning—what was it I had said? apparently. He never came up to me. I turned, once or twice, to speak to him; but he strode off. Because of him, always lurking in the offing, people even moved off before I could say a word. So I went back and sat on the steps of the Ispolkom, waiting for the little secretary to be free, so that I could being to talk horses.

I had only been sitting there a few minutes before Djhon-hote came along. He squatted, sitting on his own heels, with exquisite suppleness. He seemed at a loss for what to say. Then a hawk flew over. Did we have a bird like that where I came from he asked, brightening. Plenty, I told him. And sheep like that? Yes, we had sheep; but not sheep with these fat tails. Nor were there so many black ones. A black sheep was rare in my country, I told him; wondering would I dare make a joke on that. Then where did I come from? Originally, I answered, I came from New York. Was New

York in Berlin, he asked. No, I replied, almost floored by such innocence; New York was far, far away—on the other side of the world, in fact. I then rashly told him that while it was about nine o'clock now, where we were sitting, it was just about midnight in New York. People, some people, had already gone to bed. Then I had the mad idea to make this difference in time more dramatic. "Listen!—today is now *yesterday*—in New York." He almost got up and left me.

Still, that was the beginning. I think he thought I was always a bit touched after that. But when I went in to ask the little secretary about horses, he went to the veranda and called in Djhon-hote. We made our bargain then and there: how much he wanted each day, and—this was the only snag—how far he was willing to go with us. Time meant nothing to him, he managed to make me understand. But beyond a certain valley he would not go. "Different people" lived on the far side of it. But he would see that we got another pair of horses from them. This was all done so readily that I understood that it was an old and accepted custom of the Caucasus. We shook hands and he promised to be back with two horses in the morning. I went out on the veranda to watch him ride off. And—sure enough! —the scowling man in the good boots came up and tried to question him.

It was amusing to watch. Djhon-hote just stood there and listened to him (I was afraid it was obediently), until the surly gentleman stopped, and waited for an answer. The answer was a hearty laugh, a spit on the ground—close, insultingly close, to the immaculate boots; then Djhon-hote swung himself into the saddle of a beautiful little stallion, which he had just unhitched from the Ispolkom's rail, and trotted jauntily off. Something that he shouted back over his shoulder made one or two of the Tartars laugh, but most of them walked off silently. The wife of the little secretary was smiling when I came back to their room. "Please," she said, patting their tablecloth into order, "now you can have some more coffee."

Both she and the sore-toothed little husband seemed immensely pleased by the insolent way Djhon-hote had treated the pernicious thug. I asked the secretary how many Russians, Slavs, there were in Khassaut. "Four," he said, then quickly added—"and 402 Tartars!" I smiled, and said to him: "I think there is *one* Russian too many?" He opened his mouth wide to laugh—and groaned as his abscessed tooth reminded him it was still there.

Khassaut, at that time, could have been called a borderline community. I climbed the minaret and looked out over the tin and sod roofs to the nearby limestone crags of the mountain we had come down the night before. It would be a long time before I would forget my first look down into that mist-filled valley, and the silver river flowing under the moon. A Karachaite had climbed up and now leaned over the parapet beside me. I asked him did they still use the mosque. He nodded: it was about half full these days. Hard to get the young people to come. But I must know what young people are like—always ready to take up any new ideas. Yes, I knew, I told him: the young always get excited by new ideas. But what about the old ones, I asked him. Did they violate the Koran—and drink strong drinks? He grinned. Who doesn't? he asked me. Why, he went on, more wine was drunk at Kislovodsk than at any town in the Caucasus. And Caucasian wine was very strong, he added. Would I like some? His tongue was amost hanging out for a drink, that was evident. But I thought I would keep my good principles for a few days longer; and dug into my pocket to give him some drink money for himself. Among the coins was an English two-shilling. He asked to look at it. Was that our Tsar, he asked, pointing at the head of George V. No, I told him, something better than a Tsar. This was a *King*. Did we want to get rid of him? I shook my head. Not in the least; we hoped he would live to a good ripe old age. And then would there be another king? Of course, I said: there was one already ready. He shook his head: "Just like it always was—eh?" I had the great pleasure of being able to say YES!

And as for him and his people, I asked, was life better now? He nodded his head emphatically. As well he might! For under the Russification of the Tsars, enforced by the Cossacks, these Karachaites, once one of the fiercest races in the Western Caucasus, had been forced back and penned into the bronze rock valleys. Their good lands had been given to the Cossacks. Now, so Moscow had promised, these fine lands were going to be given back to them. And had I not seen the posters in the Ispolkom? All the big tractors at work, wheat waving, far as you could see; and all the laughing, happy men and women! (Irritating posters!) Yes, I said soberly, I had seen them. I left the minaret to go and find Wicker. I put on my shoes which I had left at the door of the mosque, and as I passed the mountaineers on the dirt road I wondered if they were not much happier with their bullocks and handlooms, all the skill of their harness- and saddle-making, rather than with the tractor and as slaves to a machine in some factory. There they would lose real freedom. It pleased me to think that this tribe of horse and cattle breeders still had a long, long climb ahead of them up the hill of so-called progress.

VII

THE little spring of sparkling Narzan at Khassaut was across the river above the mosque. I went up there the next morning before breakfast, crossed over on the foot-log, and had a good sponge bath. It was a marvellous sensation, the bubbles bursting all over me, but the water was cold as ice. The rising sun was casting long shadows from the peaks behind me and the cluster of mountains up at the far end of the valley was a pure turquoise blue. I had forgotten to bring a towel and was sitting there with my shirt off, drying off, until I finished a cigarette, when I noticed that I was holding up the day's work of the community. These Caucasian Mohammedans, according to their own customs, are very proper people; about half a dozen young girls were waiting awkwardly on the opposite side of the small river, until this half-naked man left their water-hole. They smiled and burst into outright laughter when they saw me nearly slip off the foot-log, which was very slippery from the dew. Then they walked across it like cats on a fence. They were in bare feet, of course.

While we were having breakfast, a ten-egg omelette, the President of the Khassaut Ispolkom and his wife came in. Neither of them could speak a word of Russian. She was a Persian type, slim, with an oval face, wearing a vivid red dress. She had brought us a present, a big wooden bowl of rich sour cream—*smetana*. We ate this with our tea and eggs. The night before, our chicken had been cooked with *smetana*, and the secretary of the Ispolkom, his wife, and a Tartar, all eating from the same plate by our side, scooped up the *smetana* with loud sucking noises. Best chicken I ever ate in Russia. This morning the young secretary had an automatic, which he seemed to be handling with a dreadful unfamiliarity. I asked him had he ever used it. He said no; he didn't know whether it would even go off. I took it from him and saw that it was a Spanish weapon, made by *Beistgui Hermanos*, 1914. It was rusty and, to me, looked

He was a superb creature . . . a Mongol aristocrat and this pile of rocks behind us, really a stone igloo, was the only home he had ever known in his life

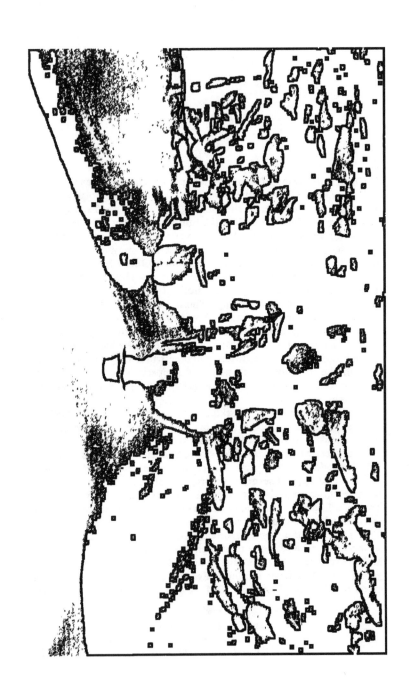

equally deadly from both ends. I told him he had better not try to see whether it would go off or not. But he had to carry it, he protested; he was going over the range to Kislovodsk that morning, and would be carrying the village taxes and the state percentage from yesterday's horse and cattle auction. He was also going to get his tooth pulled.

We got our kit out on the veranda. As in Spain, the whole village had turned up to see us set off. That is, all the males. While I was sitting there on the Ispolkom steps waiting for Djhon-hote, I had to answer the same barrage of questions that Djhon-hote had wanted to know the answer to the day before. The question of meridian time still bothered them. Was it true what I had said yesterday, that people were just now going to bed? Had I said that, in America, today was still yesterday? It certainly was, I told them. Then I thought I would give them a new aspect of time: "Over there," I said, pointing towards the rising sun, "in China—it is now tomorrow." Some of them gave me a sickly grin. But the rest just shook their heads and laughed at me: I *was* a joker!

Wicksteed, in shorts, came out and caused another avalanche of questions about his bare knees. Did the English dress like that? Yes, I told them; in India, Africa—wherever it was hot. "But it isn't hot *here*!" they cried, pointing to the snows falling on Little Bermamoot (8,500 feet). I told them Wicksteed was a warm-blooded animal.

Djhon-hote turned up, in great form, full of the high spirits of getting off, and introduced us to two horses—Kolya, a fine black stallion that he had ridden in on; and Marusha, who became our pack-horse. She looked a philosophic animal. He was rather surprised that I, the young one, was going to ride; and that it would be "Dadushka!" (old grandfather), which he immediately began to call Wicksteed, who was going to walk. We filled Kolya's saddle bags with all they would hold that we wanted to get at easily; a big black *burka* was rolled up and lashed back of the soft-pummelled saddle. This was the first time we had to decide just how we would pack. I found the typewriter and small suitcase of mine very difficult. Marusha was loaded with duffle-bag, two bedrolls, and Wicker's rucksacks. (I carried my trout rod, in its wooden case, in about fourteen different ways on that trip). None of this first packing looked too good to me. Anyway, we were off. And were we not!

I might say that after the picture had been taken of our departure (photo facing p. 48), old Wicksteed immediately set off. He liked doing things like that; he wanted to feel independent. Just himself and the mountains. "You'll find me somewhere along the road," he said casually, striding off with his long staff like any pilgrim. "I'll stick to the river." Kolya burst like a rocket when I swung up on him, scattered the spectators, and I kept him at a full gallop to take all the fizz out of him that I could. During that time I found that the soft Caucasian saddle is soft only in appearance. It is built over wood, ridged like a sharp roof; and just in the most inconvenient place there is a hard rawhide knot which gouged out an open sore in my behind before that very first day was over. It bothered me, greatly, until the day when I finally patted little Kolya lovingly on the nose, gave him a palmful of sugar, and said good-bye to him.

After a couple of miles I brought Kolya up and waited for Djhon-hote; and when he didn't turn up, I went back for him. As I had expected, he was repacking Marusha. The whole load had shifted. The duffle-bag was the culprit. His own kit was practically nil; so I flattened out the duffle-bag a bit by shifting as much as I could into his two almost empty saddle bags. And as the days went on and tin by tin the stores in the duffle vanished it became more and more amenable to being flattened out. It was a sunny day and I walked with Djhon-hote along the river bank. About half an hour, and I saw something shining in the stream ahead. It was old Wicker's skull. There he was sitting, the stream rushing around him, smoking, wearing his long-distance spectacles. "Come in," he said, "the water's fine."

It was ice. "I make it a principle," he smiled, as we sat there drying ourselves in the sun, "never to pass up a good place to bathe on the chance that there might be a better place later on. Usually there isn't." He chuckled. "On the boat—don't deny it—you thought that I was in need of a bath. Well—see that water!—I am going to have at least one good wallow in these clear mountain streams every day. I *love* the Caucasus. Makes you young."

We climbed steadily through alpine valleys. They were carpeted with wild flowers; buttercups, forget-me-nots, dandelions—and clusters of white blossoms like stars. Little Bermamoot was threatening to lose itself in a snowstorm again. But it was warm in the valleys filled with sun. In a birch spinney we put up a bird like a grouse which thundered away from us, that made Kolya nearly throw me.

Near the top of the pass we were overtaken by a militiaman, gun strung across his back and a sword strapped to his waist. He was a Kabardine. A Tartar was with him. And they both wore black *burkas*. (See photo facing p. 49). We unloaded Marusha and had lunch. Our horses, hobbled, wandered across the flowered grass. A little colt that was with the two strangers lay down and rolled on its back. Then it sighed and went to sleep. I was glad of the rest, for the hole that was worn by that knot was already beginning to smart. We lay there thinking of the fine days that lay ahead.

Looking down from the pass the green uplands folded like the roll of soft seas up to the grey buttresses that rose ahead. Clouds drifted slowly over them. They were so smooth and bare and steady green that I was fascinated to watch the islands that the cloud-shadows made in passing over them. See them darkening and turning bright green again. Beneath the clouds, in the far distance, was the hard grey of cliff faces, coursed with gullies, with snow in their ravines. I gave the militiaman and the Tartar some cigarettes and we went on.

Sometimes these cloud effects were stupendous—a tumult; billows of flaming colours. As if, say, some huge warehouse was on fire, and a floor had crashed inside the walls—and billows of fiery smoke were poured out. All these colours of fire ; rose, apricot, and the reflection thrown up by the sun shining on snowfields. And—always—when hail or the clouds did not block it out, we could turn in some direction and see snow. We were always reminded that this was the *Frosty* Caucasus.

In the upper valleys we began to come on an occasional shepherd —he was always mounted—sitting placidly on his horse, wrapped cheek and jowl against the shrill winds. It was not until then that I began to realise what a treasure a really good *burka* can be. Like army kit, these things have been tried out by the Caucasians in action— against all weathers, all circumstances. They are made from the long hair of the Caucasian black sheep. The value of the *burka* depends upon the length of the hair. A real Karachaite swell in his square-shouldered *burka* looks like a stretched-out bear's skin. When the wind blows from the left, the *burka* is lapped so that the opening is from the right; *vice versa* for the wind when it comes from the other side; if the wind is straight in a man's face, the *burka* is worn back-to-front, with the opening behind. They never *sit* on it; it stretches, as ordinarily worn, from the shoulders of the wearer, back over the saddle bags, etc., to the horse's tail. It means the maximum of comfort for both man and animal. Djhon-hote had brought two along. And we already knew that we had found a treasure in him. These shepherds always rode up to us and leaned over to shake hands. They always asked the same questions: Whence? Whither? And why?

Other horsemen appeared occasionally, galloping along the steep slopes—no other horsemen would do it. And when three of them met beside me (see photo facing p. 64) they charged their horses into each other, just for the fun of it. I was nearly finished in a scrum of squealing, kicking Caucasian horses. To make things worse, one of them, a magnificent aquiline-faced Tartar (or Turk), in walnut-brown *tcherkasska* and boots soft as gloves, insisted on a race along the mountainside. I was not so keen, but Kolya was. My horse shot after the other horse—Allah! Nothing but the Prophet could have been holding me in that deceitfully soft-pummelled Caucasian saddle. I knew I would watch all circus performances with greater interest from then on. Kolya did a flying leap over a small stream—and fetched up short. My head hit his. . . .

When I got the stars out of my eyes, I suggested to this descendant of Genghis Khan that we smoke a cigarette. When I opened my case the wind blew three of them out on the ground. Without an effort—I had watched him pick a flower that way in full gallop—my friend leaned down from his saddle and picked up two of the cigarettes. As he reached farther out from the horse to get the third, his girth slipped—but, with his hand already on the ground, he came out of the saddle and landed on his feet as lightly as a cat. He looked very embarrassed.

It began to look as if we would have a nasty night. A sleet storm suddenly struck us as we were coming into the upper range at, we estimated, about 6,000 feet. It came out of nowhere. Just before it did, I saw the Central Caucasus riding under a low bank of clouds. A lower layer seemed to be coming up their ravines. The base of the upper clouds was a straight line the entire length of the range. Between the two were the hard greys and snows of the ravines. Djhon-hote, who stared at this prospect with respect, said that this bank of clouds was seldom off the Central Range during the daylight. Then the rain hit us. Hail stones. I dismounted and we three crouched under the two *burkas*. We had just passed a band of Karachaites on trek. They had asked me for cigarettes. When I gave the headman two he gave one to a baby he had lashed to his saddle—to stop its crying. We saw them, all humped up, on the ridge behind us. Then there was the sun and the cold wind again.

We made camp well before sunset that day. I wanted to see how my improvised Fortnum and Mason pup-tent would really work. We found a shelter at a patch of stream in the mountainside, where it had flattened out. And a dry stretch of gravel backed by a stand of stunted pine gave us the two things we wanted: wood and water; and rich pasture for the horses. While Djhon-hote collected firewood, I cut two saplings for our tent uprights, and whittled some tent-pegs from an old dead branch that withstood all the hammering we gave them all the way to Mt. Elbruz. I made some rice cakes, with jam, over a cheery little campfire that faced the reddening western sky. And, of course, pot after pot of coffee in its embers. The tent worked beautifully: that is, it stood up. The only difficulty was to get into it. We slept with our heads in and feet facing the fire, of course. The front of the tent was open, about three feet high; the slope to the back left us only about a couple of clear inches over our heads. We made this clearance by placing stones, or a log whenever we could find one, under the rubber groundsheet at the back, and then pegging it down. I got into my flea-bag and hopped in backwards, like an insect carrying its shell with it. Old Wicker couldn't do that with his comforter sewn to his kapok mattress. I taunted him:

"Clever woman, that—eh, Wicker?—always trying to marry you. How did you escape her?"

"Oh, well," he grunted as he gave a convulsive heave. "She went about it quite adroitly"—heave; another groan and contortion—"but I managed to conceal my amusement. I—eh!—I said to her: 'You know, a watched pot never boils.' And she said"—a convolution of Wicker that nearly knocked the tent over—"she said: 'That's nonsense. It does if there's any fire under it.' Just to bait me, you know. Make me feel my age. And—uh——!"

"You wait till you get bedded in," I said.

"Well," he said finally, "I took her up on that very point; I just said plainly: 'Look here! I'm too old to have any of the fun out of being married, and now I'm jolly well not going to have any of its responsibilities.' "

"And that did the trick?"

"Yes. That settled it. But there was *another* woman, you know!" His voice suddenly became animated. "Ah! *She* said that it would not be necessary to get married. . . . Free love, you know. But then," he sighed—"*She* was a Russian."

"They are like that!"

"Yes, one of my pupils—my class in English, you know—he said to me: 'When a Russian lady wishes for a man she is very diligent to obtain him.'" We finally fell asleep. The fire died. Djhon-hote slept rolled in his *burka*, his saddle for his pillow, as Caucasian raiders have done throughout the ages. Sunrise was glorious.

VIII

A DAY that had begun in sunshine and romance was ending in desperation. Murky clouds veiled the lower ranges of the Caucasus; hail cut us in the face.

Twice we had stopped: once, when we had seen an encampment of Karachaite shepherds, hoping to find shelter—only to find them sitting stoically in their *burkas* beside out-spanned carts full of pain-immune women and squalling children; and again, when unable to stand the lash of the sleet, we had dumped all our duffle on the ground and squatted on it, huddled under the two felt *burkas* that we possessed between the three of us.

With my clothes sticking to me I reflected dolefully on the lives of the Caucasian mountaineers. Two hours back, we had heard that bee-like braying of lambs and had seen a mountain *kosh*, huddled on a ledge in the lower hills, a sod and stone hut where the Karachaites house themselves when they spend their summer months with their flocks. Djhon-hote suggested that we had better turn and drop down to it. Old Wicksteed, however, insisted on continuing our pilgrimage—there would be another *kosh* farther on. There must be; these mountains must be full of *koshes*, said that stubborn old man. So two hours, with Wicksteed slipping and slackening; Djhon-hote beginning to mutter; and we found a Karachaite in the clouds.

Yes, he said, there was a *kosh* "down below". He was driving four bulls. There is no use dwelling on it, that wretched trek along the mist-drenched ridge and mountainside, with my shoes squelching water from the stirrups—and the shepherd, wrapped in *burka* and *bashlik*, riding ahead of us. This was one of the times when I begged, almost cried, to make old Wicksteed take my seat on the horse. No! No! Nothing could make him do it. So he staggered and slid. And Djhon-hote, who saw a warm fire in prospect, walked jauntily beside Marusha in our rear.

Then the shepherd began to zig-zag his horse down the slippery grass mountainside; I heard the squalling of lambs; and there, down below, I saw a few circles of stone—and a long mound of sod, from which came some blue smoke. A *kosh*! There was a mountain stream down there, and a gully with a single log across it for a bridge. And as we halted, wondering whether to ride our horses through the water, which was literally jumping from rock to rock, or to try to lead them across that slippery foot-log, a group of hooded men, stooping, emerged from the stone wall of the *kosh*.

Their faces were hard, almost blackened by the snow and suns; high cheeked and generous mouthed. And very solemn. And their hands, as we shook them—each one in turn—were rough and dirty. This, it was quite apparent, was a ceremony that we had to comply with. You cannot ride out of a cloud and into a *kosh*—not without being invited. They eyed us.

We were asked to come in. I rode my horse down the gully, through the swirling water, and up the bank. Then I left it. As a guest of the *kosh* I daren't do anything more. They unloaded for us, they carried in our bags. They beat off the fierce dogs that flew at us—and we found ourselves inside a low stone hut that was as dark as a tunnel. The smoke brought tears to our eyes. . . .

Then these Karachaites ran for more firewood; they threw on logs that they must have carried for miles, as these smooth mountain slopes bear no timber. The *kosh* flamed. The heat of the flames started upward and outward currents of hot air that also sucked the smoke out. There was no chimney, no window; the fire was just laid on the dirt floor against the stone wall. The smoke was sucked out through a hole in the sod roof. And as the flames rose I saw a ring of dark faces staring at me. An old woman, her head wrapped in a scarf like a turban; an oval-faced girl, who was leaning forward trying to pull off my boots; a row of children, dirty with soot beyond all description. And the face of my host! To see a face like *that*—lit by the flames; Semitic, and savage, and—smiling. . . . He had his youngest child between his knees. It had been eating sour cream, its face was covered with it—and the father was now cleaning its hands by rubbing them with his own.

He sat there on a stump of a log beside his hearth, watching us intently for fear that we might not find pleasure in it, find it too humble, while his women-folk brought us wooden bowls of sour cream, cheese, and slabs of the soggy, pale Caucasian maize bread.

· 92 ·

Utsch-Kalan, capital of Karachay

Their bed, the communal bed, was a litter of fibre, like sisal, piled in one corner, from which the whole family had cleared so that we might lie down. They sat amongst saddles and tubs of sour milk, the women in the shadows, as we men passed the bowl of sour cream from mouth to mouth. We all drank deep. Not to have shown signs of enjoying it would have been the greatest discourtesy. And if I had not seen that child's face smeared with sour cream, I think I would have enjoyed it; but I could not get rid of the idea that its sooty face had been at this bowl of cream first. The soot dropped from the birch-saplinged roof whenever we hit it with our heads. One has to crawl when inside a *kosh*. As the flames mounted we had to lie farther back on our sleeping bags which we had spread out on the sisal. From being half frozen we were now almost being scorched. A craggy-featured Karachaite sat beside me. His repose, so silent, was like that of a cat which sits beside you and begins to clean itself when it is content. Then a girl crawled across and held a copper urn while he washed his hands and feet. Then he knelt and began to pray. He bowed and touched his head to the ground, twice. Then he arose again, as much as he could in the *kosh*, murmuring his prayers, and then got down on his knees and touched his head to the earth again. An orthodox Mohammedan, he had propitiated Allah—and now we could discuss our dinner.

In the shadows (the Mohammedan women are always there) two girls were making butter by shaking cream back and forth in a goat-bladder. The two sopping wet bandages on my left leg had to be changed. It was embarrassing, but I must say I enjoyed the awe, the consternation which I caused when I dropped a few crystals of potassium permanganate into the bowl of clear water. That fascinated them. This was magician's work! I carried a whole kit of medicine, bandages, etc., in my small suitcase; together with some five hundred sheets of paper on which I hoped to type my stories, at Utsch-Kalan or Teberda, and send them off to justify this trip. Now all these primitive and likeable faces formed a ring as I swabbed out the bone of my shin and foot and dusted some iodoform in the two open wounds. Now they were certain that I was a healer.

The immediate result was a small Karachaite boy, who was brought in from a neighbouring *kosh*. His finger had been crushed between a tree and a rock a month before. It was a shocking sight. The whole tip of the left index finger was a mass of proud, suppurating flesh—and out of it protruded the bone. I almost gasped. I unpacked my medical kit again, boiled some more water, and repeated the miracle of turning it purple. While I was waiting for it to cool I felt the lymphatic glands in the boy's arm. I felt under his armpit. Did that hurt, I asked him. He shyly shook his head. This little hero was utterly impassive. He made me feel ashamed of myself for the secret satisfaction I had enjoyed by the potassium permanganate miracle. I made him hold his poor finger in the warm water until it was cold. Then I dressed it as best I could.

Their idea of sepsis was terrifying. When I threw the pus-covered rag which had been around his finger into the fire, a woman, presumably his mother, seized it. She rolled it into a ball and then picked up her baby, whose bottom was bare, and sat him on that gory mess, whereupon she contentedly began to rock him. I trembled for the little boy with the smashed finger.

This was serious, I said to Djhon-hote, asking him to translate for me. I said that the boy might lose his hand, even his arm, if they did not get him to a doctor at once. Take him to Kislovodsk—tomorrow. This caused a dispute. Then the old man, the Old Man of the Tribe, the one who had been praying, said a few words which silenced all of them. Sitting on his haunches, he bowed solemnly to me. The boy would be taken to Kislovodsk in the morning, translated Djhon-hote. I think I saved that one arm in the Caucasus. But I did not know what I had let myself in for. Djhon-hote spread the news, wherever we arrived, that he was travelling in the company of a learned man, a great healer. And everything maimed, sick, even *malade imaginaire* was brought to me. When one tribe brought a woman forward who had no nose—just a rotting red hole in her face—I almost needed a doctor myself. Such was the price of fame.

The old man of the *kosh* killed a lamb (which ceremonial I shall describe to you later on), and as we sat there eating the hot meat from the iron pot I glimpsed a calf in the section of *kosh* next to me— there were five families, divided by wattled walls; and in one beyond I heard a cream-separator going! Cream from the separator (Swedish), and butter made in a bladder. Our host gave us his bed and the best bits of meat—his wife or wives and daughters ate what was left—and this was where West met East. He gave it to us, that sheep; almost sacrificial in its ceremony. Although he would not deign to mention it, it was obviously in gratitude for what I had done for the young boy with the injured hand. From there on we bought sheep; and, once their pride was at stake, we found the Karachaites the most ferocious bargainers. They would even show us one fat little black lamb, and then. when we had finally agreed on the price, after, say, an hour's wrangle, they would even try to substitute another and inferior lamb when they came to kill it. Much like the *maître d'hôtel* who displays the fine salmon-trout for your approval, then serves its baby brother. Wicker and I had made up our minds, the Lord alone knows how we arrived at the price, that we would pay seven roubles for a sheep. No more and no less. And strange as it may seem, we got a sheep for that price all the way across the Caucasus.

We lay there on the sisal, leaning back against our saddles; and the oval-faced girl who had tried to pull off my wet boots for me, obviously the most sophisticated, or least afraid, of the lot, began a fluttering little song. Djhon-hote, and then the men in the *kosh*, joined in to hum in different keys. Then they sang another song. The songs always ended in sadness; the notes broke and fluttered away—like falling leaves. Only one song had a lilt to it, and I asked what it was. A girl answered that it was to her young husband (she had a face like the Vladimir Madonna), and he, laughing at such absurdity, translated it to me· it was the Song of Freedom of Mohammedan women under the Soviets—the new life.

Then I noticed that he was dressed differently from the rest. When he sat upright from the dark shadows in which he had been lying, paying no attention to us, rather fed up, I believe, of the notoriety I was achieving because of my attention to the young boy, I saw that he had on a Sam Browne belt and a revolver. These proclaimed him, instantly, as a Communist. He began by being good-natured, or good-mannered. He started by asking me where I came from, and then, like the other Karachaites, asked me if New York was in Berlin. No, I said. And neither did I agree with him that Hoover, out of desperation, would recognise the Soviets just at present. He had some very badly digested Moscow propaganda inside his handsome head. I was rather admiring him, when I saw he was a young Communist, as a life-line from the old Karachaite life to the new. Until he said:

"You are not a Communist—eh? Well, you understand: unless America recognises the Soviets—if you are not a Communist—you will not be allowed into the U.S.S.R.!"

"And without American engineers to build your factories and show you how to make things, without Colonel Cooper to build your big Dnieper dam for you—who do you think is building that dam, anyway?" I asked him—"there will be no U.S.S.R. Tell me—have you ever heard of Colonel Cooper?"

No, he grumbled, he had not. I smiled at him. I smiled at the *khazain*, the Old Man of the *kosh*. He looked uneasy, and stared at his young Communist son. The youth snapped a short sentence at them in Karachaite. And the Old Man, nodding with great politeness to Wicker and me, made a wave of his hand towards the hay. It was time, his gesture said, to go to sleep.

IX

WICKSTEED had been upset by the short but sharp political argument of the previous night. "It just spoils these mountains," he said morosely. "Why can't people leave each other alone?"

I told him that that would indeed be a new world. One infinitely better than that which the Bolshevik friends were trying to badger everyone into believing in. But that as far as we were concerned, if we had any sense, the Caucasus were ours for the asking. I suggested we should accept no hospitality whatsoever from now on, if we could possibly avoid it. We had our improvised pup-tent; Djhon-hote had his *burka*. We were free. And on particularly rainy or snowy nights we could use the other *burka* for a groundsheet and the rubber groundsheet to make an extra shelter that would cover all three of us. This worked splendidly—not that we were not glad to accept shelter on certain nights later on—and we saw sunrises in the Caucasus when the snows turned gold and rose that filled us with an exaltation that was almost too much to bear.

"If you can live without bed or board, and travel on boiled mutton, black bread, and sour milk," I argued, "what can there be in these mountains that can make them unpleasant for us?"

But on this morning I was determined that I was going to make that young Communist smile, and even like us, before we left. So I addressed myself to him. The *khazain*, the Old Man of the Tribe, had got up and had been praying to Mecca, of course, with the first cock-crow. It was a crystal clear morning, and after it had boiled on the embers I brought out our pot of coffee so that Wicker and I and Djhon-hote could drink it outside, where we sat spreading the soft cheese on slabs of maize bread. I called the young Communist over to us and asked him to join us and have a cigarette. Was that boy his brother, I asked him as he squatted by our side. He said no, but he would see that he would get into Kislovodsk all right; he was setting off back there himself this morning. I rinsed my cup from our canvas water-bucket and poured him some coffee. He thawed a bit as he squatted there smoking (he said the Gold Flakes were very strong—much stronger than Caucasian tobacco); and when I asked him where he had joined the Young Communist organisation, the Konsomols, and he said Rostov-on-Don, and I said that *that* was a fine city! well, everything was all right. He could not resist the temptation to tell us of his travels. But when I asked him what he intended to become, and he said: "An Instructor in Communism," I had to repress my: "Good God!" Anyway, he shook my hand with real warmth before he swung himself gracefully into his saddle, and the little boy was lifted up to ride, bare-back, behind him.

We asked about the lie of the land. We were told that this river, which came straight down from another, and higher, range of the Caucasus, had *koshes* right up to its very head. And the next valley? we said, pointing our arm in the direction of Mt. Elbruz. Nothing, said the Old Man: we would find no people there. Why? He didn't know: the people on the other side of this valley were different. He had never been over there. Probably it was a rocky valley, and the grazing was no good. Djhon-hote found the hobbled horses, which had been grazing by the stream; we re-saddled and repacked Marusha, and set off for the high ridge again. Up here when we had got clear of the steep grassy slope, there was a well-defined horse trail between the rocks and low bushes. The air was unbelievably fresh and pure. This sense of exaltation, of being completely free of man, did not leave us again until, a couple of weeks later, we dropped down, from 8,000 feet, into Utsch-Kalan on the headwaters of the Kuban. If we had been riding for time, however, we could have got there in a few days, even with old Wicker walking. But in that case we would never have gone up to the head of these rivers and streams, or camped beside them in the deserted valleys—where I hoped to get some good trout fishing. I had wired my paper, when I received permission to make this trip, that I would be at least six weeks away from Moscow.

I was already beginning to feel a strange thing about the Caucasus, this massive chain which separates Europe from Asia. They were old. Out in British Columbia, where my wife and I had lived for two years on a log houseboat on a lonely lake up in the forest of Vancouver Island, the virgin woods seemed as fresh as if they had just been made. It was like the Dawn of Creation to wander up some of those bouldered streams under the fresh, sparkling sun. On some of the streams, I am sure, none but an occasional Siwash trapper had ever been up them, or perchance some white gold prospector. At any rate, no man had ever left any evidence of his passing behind him. In this way we came on beaver dams in a part of the Island from which, it was commonly believed, the beaver had long since been exterminated. It was following a wisp of snipe that I, one day, suddenly came on my first one. High up, a considerable distance away from the big lake, on the wall of forest-clad mountain and then the grey rocks above the timber line, that had always shut us off from the, at that date (1921), almost untravelled Nitinat country. And sitting there, studying the freshly gnawed sapling stumps around the beavers' dam, admiring the skill of their tooth-and-tail work, I was aware that I was in a part of the world that had not changed, except for falling trees, for perhaps thousands of years. There was no taint of man whatsoever. And that was very encouraging. . . . Down on the big lake where I had my houseboat, I wrote thousands of words about the mountain opposite us. Its flat grey tones of winter; then the lush depths, almost the "hum" of spring, when the water, instead of showing black against the snow, was a deep, shimmering blue, and you could *feel* the pulse of the sap in every swaying rush and in the tall silent firs. I wrote about that same mountain again and again—in order to learn how to write. And through all the words, especially in the freshness and fullness of spring, came the feeling that I was in a world that had just been made. That *is* the feeling of the British Columbia forests, when you get clear away from the murderous logging camps.

But the Caucasus are old—covered with the dust of Asia. Ancient civilisations: the Kingdom of Georgia, on the other side of the main chain, and its great queen, Tamara, with life in Tiflis more advanced in the arts than was the London of that day; the Greek and Roman civilisation along the Caucasian coast of the Black Sea; Tamerlane, building his mound on the river Aras, on the spot where he had killed a lion; the Princes of Kabarda; and the Cossacks of the Line, who began their invasion of the Caucasus around the mouth of the Terek in the sixteenth century. These Russians, under the great Yermolov (who gave no quarter, even to women and children), waging their unending warfare against perhaps the most reckless and skilful riders and swordsmen in the world. Generation after generation,

Persian and Turk, surged up against this wall of the Caucasus; steadily the Russians bore down from the north. Wicker and I knew that there was not a valley we ascended, not a pass that we crossed, not a deep forest that we traversed, which had not once known the smell of hot blood from hand-to-hand fighting.

With the mountaineers, to be disarmed was to be dishonoured; and attempts to disarm them had not succeeded up to the time Wicksteed and I travelled among them. Every man carried the deadly *kindjal*, the two-foot fluted, razor-sharp dagger.

I "wasted" the greater part of that day fishing. It is seldom, as we get on, that one feels the sudden, unaccountable, bubbling happiness of youth. But I had a burst of it as we sat there in the glorious sunshine—eating our lunch, of corn bread and cheese, helped out with one of the big tins of Marchand sardines I had brought back from London—and I saw that glorious silver stream below me, rippling in the sun, jumping from rock to rock over its ledges, with the deep green pools and the overhanging thickets. I told Wicker we would make our camp by the stream that night, find an open space before I started fishing, hobble the horses so that they could graze in the deep fresh grass, and make everything shipshape before I left him and Djhon-hote. We found an open space, backed by an overhanging wall of rock, under which Djhon-hote said that he could sleep snug as a bug in a rug in his thick felt *burka*. Then I put my rod together and set off upstream. . . .

I had no waders. I was travelling light in the Caucasus, as I had learned to do long before. I had one blue flannel shirt (which I called a "thousand-miler," i.e., it didn't show dirt, and you could wear it that distance before you absolutely had to wash it), one heavy, very heavy, old Air Force flannel shirt, and two light Viyellas. On one of these I had amputated the arms at the elbows. I had a light gaberdine coat and two pairs of gaberdine breeks (Norfolk pattern), which I had had made purposely for this trip by my tailor. They buttoned tight below the knee (the left one being loose enough to take my bandage), and they were loose and baggy from the knee up. Very comfortable—but cold as hell in snow and rain, as I was to discover almost every day. However, they dried quickly. An old battered Harris tweed coat and a pair of new flannel bags. A good dozen thick socks, and a pair of tough Scotch brogues. For books I carried *Taras Bulba, The Cossacks, On a Chinese Screen* (as a model to work

Headwaters of the Kuban where I got thirty-five trout

vignettes from), and Gorky's *Through Russia*. I only wish to goodness I had read, and had with me, Lermontov's *A Hero of Our Times* for then I would have walked out, at Kislovodsk, and seen the ledge from which the pitiless Petchorin killed Grouchnitzky in the duel.

I had a duplex Abbey and Imbre American trout rod, a splendid bit of work, which could be used for either fly or spinner. And the two reels I always carried with it. This rod, with its alternative joints, was carried in a slotted wooden cylinder, tied to my saddle—and very nearly cost me my life in the Caucasus. As we were zig-zagging down a mountain face of sheer rock, on the most harrowing of narrow ledges, it caught in the wall of the cliff and nearly pronged the horse and me off the ledge. After that I knew enough to shift it to the outside whenever we came to narrow places, of which there were plenty.

Nearly all these streams are made from glaciers, some springing almost full-grown from beneath the glacial face, all made from the deep reservoirs of snow in the shell-shaped cirques up above. And what had looked so enticing from a couple of thousand feet above, now made me feel gloomy even as I put my rod together. The water was glacial grey, full of the pulverised rock, etc., that the moving ice, which is Nature's sandpaper, had been rubbing from time immemorial from the rocky basin up above. I got no trout. The day was coming when I got thirty-five snow trout—out of the headwaters of the Kuban, in one day—but that day lay some weeks ahead.

I had thought it almost impossible not to catch trout in the Caucasus. And Wicker and I had counted on them largely for our food. For that reason we broke our recently made resolution and decided to make friends with another set of *kosh*-living people, and buy a sheep from them. I had seen one up the river, and the next day, after a futile try at the stream again, we repacked Marusha and went along up to it. As usual, while we were talking with the Old Man outside, the women of the *kosh* had been clearing the best space on its hard dirt floor for Wicker and me to sleep on. Djhon-hote, of course, always bedded down with the rest. Then we crawled in and I broached the subject of a sheep. The Old Man said something, and his son came back in a few minutes with a middling-sized black lamb. Then the bargaining began. There is no need to go into it; perhaps our price of seven roubles, which we had determined while on the Volga, may have been pretty near what we should have given.

But it was obvious that it would be no fun at all for the Old Man if he couldn't shake us. But we also wanted to impress Djhon-hote with our firmness, so he would tell any other shepherds that we came to, to buy a sheep, that we knew what we wanted, and would pay no more. In one or two instances farther on it took well over an hour's wrangling to get a sheep, took so long that we went through the motions of going to bed, without any dinner—whereupon we got the sheep.

It was a gory performance, and it was always the same. Once the price had been agreed upon, the sheep was brought in alive and held up for our inspection, just as the waiter will bring you a live trout in a London or Paris restaurant. Then the Old Man of the tribe pulled his fluted dagger out of its silvered case, and deftly cut its throat. This was done inside the low stone *kosh*, the whole bizarre scene of strange, staring faces, silvered saddles and bridles, and Wicker's bald head and long beard lighted up by the log fire. The women drained the sheep's blood into a bladder and hung it up. Inside every *kosh* or log cabin that we were to come to was this upright tree trunk, with one branch remaining that had been sharped into a spike. The Old Man, sticking one of the sheep's hind legs through the other, as you would a rabbit's, with a few deft strokes severed its head and pulled its skin off it like a shirt. He cut off the head and handed it to the children, who stuck a stick up its nostrils and began to toast it over the fire. Then while the girls were stripping the entrails and tying them into bunches, like bundles of macaroni (for use later as catgut, probably) the Old Man took an axe and split the sheep. When the axe got too bloody, he wiped it on his boot.

Then we cooked that delicious sheep. The head we always gave to the people who had owned the animal. They ripped its lower jaw off, split the skull with an axe, to get at the brains, and then made it into soup.

With a prong of a green stick we toasted the chops, or saddle, of that sheep over the fire. Mountain sheep are sweet as nuts. And these Caucasian sheep were as succulent as those I had gorged on in the high Pyrenees, when I was riding a mule down the Basque country on the Spanish side. But here in the Caucasus we had an added delight—as our bits of sheep were toasting and the fat nicely crackling over the rose embers, we took them aside for a moment and pushed them in a bowl of sour cream, then we held them back to toast. Sometimes we made *shaslik*, cutting the bits of meat into chunks and then spearing them on a green wand between chunks of fat. The hind legs we placed each in a separate waxed canvas bag that I had had made in London, together with the remainder of the meat, and bound tightly at the neck with a hard cord. This was to prevent the flies getting at the meat and "blowing" it. These waxed bags were carried either from my saddle or tied to Marusha's pack. A sheep treated this way lasted us a good three days.

The maize cakes in this *kosh* were hot and light. We drank our usual gallon of coffee, sharing it with the others. Then we lay at full length by the fire and smoked. It was a grand sight, with the silvered saddlery and weapons, and, without being able to say a word to any one of them, it was accepted on both sides that we were friends. What a barrier language is! Then one of the girls, hidden in the darkness, began to sing. It was like a high, whining cry—something that came out of the everlasting steppe, out of Asia. You will hear that high Asiatic note, this plaintive cry, in the ballet music of Rimsky-Korsakov. It holds immense distance, and sadness, and longing, and ancient memories in its tones, and it was not hard, drowsy by that dying fire, to imagine I was seeing the Golden Horde moving across the mounded plains by the Amur river. The mood in the Caucasus is almost always of early Mongol days.

We had had our own saddles brought in, of course; and using mine as a back-rest, with my feet toward the fire, I fell asleep sitting up. I was full of mutton and completely satisfied with life. They did not wake me.

When I crawled out in the morning to greet the *khazain*, a yellow dog, about the size of a wolf and much the same build, flew at me. With his snarling rush, and his lips pulled back, he looked unstoppable. He received a clunk on the nose from the son that sounded like a club hitting a hollow coconut. I learned that these dogs are trained to fly at all strangers, as they did at us all over the Caucasus; there are a couple of heavy sticks always leaning against the wall of each *kosh*, to hit them with when they fly at a guest. They seem not to take it amiss. This dog put his tail between his legs and slunk off. How they ever survive such vicious blows on the snout was a puzzle to us. They were unquestionably the most ferocious domestic animals I have ever encountered. But they are rattling good watch-dogs!

Many of the Caucasian streams come straight from the glaciers of the main chain, cutting their way through the lower parallel ranges in deep gorges. The grass of these alps is always covered with brightly coloured flowers, that decrease in size but seem to increase in vivid colouring as you go up. Lying down on the grass, to rest in the warm sun, you are suddenly amazed to see the richness of these minute bright bits of colour all around you. Above the grass-line is always a raw path of detritus or broken stone. And up here, when it was merely raining down below, we were usually pushing ahead through a light storm of snow. The great Main Range was cut off from us while we were in these valleys of the lower ranges. The cold grey spurs that towered above us were free from snow, except that which lay in their deep ravines; we climbed over the ridge out of our valley that day, crossed a small stream by fording, and for the rest of the day worked down along it, lashed by a hailstorm in the early part of it, which followed us until we got into a deep patch of pine forest down below. The stream, rapidly growing larger, was rushing past us all the time, foaming over its shale ledges. We could see nothing at all of the mountain down which we had come, as it had its heads in the clouds, as did that of an opposite mountain, which thus formed a gap. We could see the snow fields in its serrated ravines, but had no idea of its height or what lay beyond that gap. We found an old abandoned *kosh*, built against a large wall of rock, in an open space in the forest, and camped in that. Because of the rain we stayed there two days.

We made camp one night in an abandoned *kosh*, in a mysteriously deserted valley at the foot of the Main Range. It seemed almost ominous that no one was living there. It was rich with good grass, lush and deep; and Kolya and Marusha, after we had hobbled them, had only to make a few jumps to eat their clever little heads off. They ate all day, at halts or in motion; it was a pleasure to watch them, and the companionship with the animals was certainly one of the most satisfying emotions of this trip. But Kolya, when we were negotiating a narrow ledge that morning, where his feet placed seven or eight inches to the left would have meant the end of us both—Kolya, in passing, suddenly switched round his head to snatch a wild iris. He was always thinking of his stomach: I think he left it to some sixth sense to see where his feet were going.

It was a delectable spot to camp, complete isolation. The stream, down whose valley we had been working during the usual hailstorm all morning, was still rushing past us; bigger, and coloured now from all the powdered rock washed in by the rain. Milky green. Above us towered the ridge of the main chain of the Caucasus· black rocks, and grey spurs with snow in their ravines, then an unbroken blanket of snow going up under the clouds. This was the first time we had seen the snows of the Main Range for some days.

The *kosh* was just a lean-to of rocky slabs and sod-covered saplings, placed against the face of a cliff. It had been built so long ago that the interior cliff-face and the roof-beams glistened like tar from the wood-smoke of ages: when I took out my knife and stuck it into the tar, to get some idea of how long it had taken the coating to accumulate, it went in about a quarter of an inch. God knows when the last people had been here, or what their story was: we found no signs whatever of any recent habitation. A log across the dirt floor marked where the straw beds had been. Djhon-hote, elated with such a snug shelter, started a roaring fire out of wet wood with only one gum-stick. Wicksteed took off his shorts (imagine such things in a hailstorm!) and was squatting, dressed in nothing but shoes and spectacles, before the fire. He smiled lewdly and remarked to Djhon-hote that it was just as well that this wasn't last night's *kosh* "with all those women to see me!" Djhon-hote, whose sense of the ridiculous seemed set on never letting old bearded Wicker get away with anything, rejoined instantly: "Oh, *nitchevo*—they wouldn't mind *you*, grandad!" I rummaged our food-kit, to get away from the inevitable rice-cakes, and produced a sardine-omelette, with hot corn-bread. It was about as cozy a night as one could ask for.

The entire day had been an ordeal: the sort of day when you are fatigued, wet to the skin—and love every minute of it. We had counted on making an early start, but our Mohammedan hosts had delayed us with an enormous breakfast of corn-bread, and butter we had seen them making in the goat-bladder. And then the white, tasteless cheese. The crudity of their lives is shocking at times, especially when it is raining. As we rode up the cloud-drenched valley we had seen them sitting on their desolate horses, masked to the eyes in *bashliks*, their black *burkas* dripping, standing guard over their bleating knots of fat-tailed black sheep. Karachaite boys, barefoot in the downpour, raced other horses along the steep mountainsides to round up wayward cattle. Karachaite shepherds stood guard over stone pens full of lambs.

We saw Karachaites on the march in search of better grass:

wattle-pens already up for their lambs; fresh-born foals feeding beside their hobbled mothers; drenched children watching the stupid movements of the long-horned grey cattle. Their hyena-like dogs sat dolefully under carts, morose and useless. In any other land, such as Scotland, they would have been trained into intelligent assistants and proud companions. The men, wrapped in *burkas*, sat in stolid resignation on the shafts of the awkward two-wheeled carts, carts full of women and children—sitting there, waiting until the clouds left their valley so that they could resume their eternal march. These Caucasian uplands, flowered and green, hold a miserable life when it rains.

When a mountain Karachaite comes in out of the rain it is to a smoke-filled dark hut, a bed on the dirt floor, a bowl of sour cream or curds, some soggy corn-bread—at the best, on ceremonial occasions, a few times a year, a bit of roasted sheep. He sits by the hot wood fire until the moisture steams out of his clothes; he than takes off his moccasins and fills them with fresh straw—he never wears stockings—and then he lies down to sleep, very often on just the dirt floor itself, in the same black felt *burka* that has just shielded him from rain in the hills. Drenched when it rains, that is why, perhaps, he so seldom uses water to wash with. The stream flows by; he might bathe in it—but it is unpleasantly reminiscent of the chilling rain.

But such a life was ours tonight; and for many others, we hoped. When you don't have to do it for ever that puts a different face on it. The crackling small fire that Djhon-hote had started with the invariable one gum-chip was all the more delightful because it meant refuge from the storm. Clocks and hours stop in these isolated valleys of the Caucasus. The half-side of sheep, wrapped in one of Wicksteed's shirts, would soon be purified by the flames, and turned into succulent *shaslik*. Djhon-hote was already using his long-bladed dagger for its legitimate purposes these days, hacking up the mutton to slide down a long skewer of wood. He sang as he worked, toasting the sheep over a bed of rose-red embers he had raked out from the main blaze. From time to time he took the skewered sheep away and sluiced it with salted hot water. On other embers I had a frying pan full of rice cakes. I dusted them with a little of our powdered sugar, and added some raisins.

The rice cakes were a success. Djhon-hote was fascinated by the idea of raisins in them. He picked up the hot rice directly out of the frying pan and shovelled it into his bearded mouth. His high-cheeked mountain face gleamed in the firelight, as did some escaped grains of rice in his red beard. He was a jolly chap.

"What price civilisation?" sighed Wicker as, belly full, he filled his pipe. Djhon-hote made a bed of his saddle-felts and saddle. He wrapped himself in his hairy black *burka*. The hairier it is the more expensive and distinguished—and Djhon-hote, who had gone to sleep in his fur hat, looked like a square-shouldered, very furry black bear. I threw on a few more sticks of firewood to keep the light going while we undressed, for this was the first night in the Caucasus that I had not gone to sleep with all my clothes on.

I went outside to have a last look at the night. It had stopped raining. For a time my eye was held by what I took to be an amazingly bright line of silvered clouds high in the sky, and then—"My God!" I said. I was looking at the Main Range of the Caucasus. I heard a grunt, and then a deep, satisfied chuckle behind me. "Now you know," said old Wicker, "why I love the Caucasus."

The moon was shining full on the snows of the main chain. The peaks were hard and sharp, but we could only know they were there by the white, silvered ravines of snow that led up them. Of their black upper peaks, free from snow, we could gain no concept whatever, just a fleck of white here or there. It was stupendous. Our own flowered valley was drenched with pale light. I went along to the horses and found Marusha and Kolya, munching placidly, standing deep among the lush grass by the stream. I crawled back into the warm *kosh*, undressed on my bedroll, and got into a pair of fresh and very welcome pyjamas. Then I slid down into the soft Jaeger flea-bag, and, using my warm flannel shirt for a pillow (with some sweaters for stuffing), I lay there on my side watching the fire die down as I smoked a last cigarette and jotted down in my notebook —or tried to—the almost unrecordable ecstasy I had felt when I suddenly realised that that long line of silver-white in the sky was the snows of the Main Range. I would go through many another day of rain and hail for a night like this.

X

" AH, Dedushka, Dedushka—it is a fine day!" cried Djhon-hote. "It is, without doubt, a fine day! I am happy."

Old Wicksteed, who was furious at always being called "Grandfather" by all the Cossacks and Karachaites, yet who knew it was useless to protest against anything so universal, crawled out of the *kosh* like a surly bear. I gave him a shove; I, too, wanted to enjoy the fine day, and my first cloudless view of the Main Range of the Caucasus. There it lay, its snows sparkling in the sun. A view of indescribable freshness, it seemed to fill the whole world with joy—and peace. Kolya and Marusha were feeding complacently in the sun. I don't suppose they had stopped eating all night, nor did they seem to have moved forty feet. The night had been bitterly cold, which we began to find out the minute the fire died; I envied Wicker his kapok mattress and little home-made sleeping bag. I felt that my own hip-bones were going to come through the flesh; I also felt, with a congealing spine, every chink in the loosely piled *kosh*. I lighted a candle to go on with my notes. Through the broken wattles on either side of us, I saw the cattle pens of this primitive dwelling's former inhabitants; and I pondered, a bit enviously, over the idea that when this *kosh* had been full of its rightful inhabitants, with calves, lambs, and humans, if their combined animal heat did not take the edge off this iciness? Old Wicksteed, artful even in his sleep, had rolled over, and, with instinctive thoughtfulness, pulled my half of the heavy felt Karachaite rug off me. I pulled it back, took a good look at his old bearded face, just to see that he really was asleep and had not done that on purpose, and went on with my notes. I fell asleep about dawn, and therefore it seemed I had hardly closed my eyes before I heard Djhon-hote's shouts outside that it was a fine day. He was wearing my brogues again.

He had used my soap the day before, without asking my permission; now he asked for my razor. I repeated what I had told him

Shoeing a horse in the high Caucasus

the first day I met him, back in Khassaut—and how far back that seemed now, and how far we three had gone in getting to know each other!—then I said derisively: "Where on your face could you use a razor!" Unabashed, he put his hand on my arm, called me "Darling!" and asked for a cigarette. There were blue gentians by the stream, buttercups, and I placed my metal mirror on a rock to shave in ice-cold water.

I saw that the northern slope of this valley, which caught most of the sun was forested with scrub oak. Its glades were bright with lilies and a white star-like flower which I did not know. While I got the breakfast, Djhon-hote, singing happily some wild Caucasian chant which I also did not know, "ironed out" the rawhide bridles by stropping them around a birch tree (see reins of the two horsemen, facing p. 64). They were still soggy from yesterday's rain and drying in curls. I made him deliver my brogues. My surgical felt boot was also still damp and soggy; and I resolved to ride with one stockinged foot on such a sunny day, and I put the inevitable fresh dressings on my leg while old Wicker and Djhon-hote cleaned up after breakfast. We were at about 7,000 feet then, and in a few days were going to top a pass that was 9,800.

We regretted to leave such a friendly, lonely spot, where we seemed to feel a fellowship with every blade of grass or tree. Wicker suggested that I try some fishing, but the water was grey, glacial, and I told him that I did not think it would be worthwhile even to put my rod together. (This was a mistake, as I found farther on.) This valley had a feeling of utmost repose, compared to former nights when we had slept in *koshes*. But the last hitch was thrown. Our supply of mutton was safe in its waxed bags tied to my saddle (so I thought), and we set off to descend the rest of the valley. We were making for where this river was joined by another, up whose valley we intended to climb.

The valley was dotted with mountain birch, gnarled and glistening in the warm sun. The snow peaks behind us were blazing white. We got down to a notch, where another river flowed past us, joining ours to become, I suppose, another main tributary of the Terek, which ultimately flowed into the Caspian. It was a large thought to ponder upon.

We stripped here in the warm sun and Wicker and I had a quick swim, and then put on some dry clothes and let our other ones, still damp, dry out thoroughly on the warm sands. It was a lovely spot for a doze, with a few sand-pipers to keep us company. We had unsaddled and unloaded the horses, and did not bother to hobble them. I tried for some trout again, and again had no luck. The water of this stream was greenish and slow; either it was not glacial or it had deposited its silt a long way back. But not a trout did I rise. Then we loaded the horses again and set off up the new valley.

It was about 6,000 feet up here, we estimated, where these two streams met, and we camped that night about a thousand feet above it. It was about as pleasant a day as we were to spend in the Caucasus; filled with a physical, purely animal delight, which came from an entire day of warm sun. The delightful thing about these forests of mountain birch is that they have no underbrush. It is just the woods of thick, gnarled birch rising from the rich grass. The shadows lie dark on the green floor. The bright green of the birch leaves is fresh and delicate. Blue butterflies flit underneath, floating over thickets of azaleas in the glades, lawns of buttercups and wild roses. These valleys seem too felicitous for the "wild" Caucasus.

On one of these nights, I can't remember which, except that our campfire lighting up the under branches of the pines around us made me think nostalgically of my days in western Canada, I asked Wicker to get the leg of sheep out of its waxed bag and hand it to me. He took suspiciously long; I saw that he was dusting it, and when I got up to take it from him he backed off toward the stream. When I got it away from him and brought it back to the fire, I saw that it had been fly-blown and was simply alive with maggots. I threw it in the stream. "My God!" he cried in real grief—"you've thrown away our *dinner*!" "You beat me," I laughed; "would you really have eaten that?" "Certainly!—what's a fried maggot?"

In one birch glade we found an encampment of Tartars, some of the ugliest people I have ever looked at, squatting about in a little paradise of azaleas and tiger lilies. They were smaller than any of the tribesmen we had seen so far, much more Mongol in appearance, and I think they must have been Nogai Tartars, who used to join with the Crimean Tartars in their raids on Moscow. They were very friendly. They told us that they had halted for a rest and were then taking their livestock over the mountains to fresh pasture. Goats, sheep, and cattle were dozing in little islands of horns and hide. Mothers were suckling their children; the men, in the broad black felt hats that some tribesmen wear in summer, were sleeping where they lay. They roused themselves when we came on the scene; one of them poured us out some sour milk from a skin. In return, I had to watch a half tin of Gold Flakes disappear in a flash. Then they grinned, sat on their heels, and watched us make camp.

We went on with them for the next two days. They told Djhon-hote that they knew the way through the mountains to Utsch-Kalan, the capital of Karachay; they were going part of the way themselves. They were very slow-moving owing to the impossibility of getting the small animals across deep streams. We forded one the next morning, at a point they led us to; Wicksteed sitting on Kolya behind me, Djhon-hote sitting on Marusha's rump, almost in the water. The bulk of the tribe led the sheep and goats higher up the valley, to where the stream was smaller, and did not rejoin us until nearly sunset. There was a long trail along a mountain edge, leading to another valley, along which they said we must go; and then, suddenly—we were on a road.

Sandy and grass-grown, but undoubtedly a road. It was almost cloying, after the freshness of the deserted valleys. A stream raced beside it, grey with débris, and we plodded along upwards again. This led to a broad bare plateau, backed by a rim of mountains, and here we halted for the night. The bronze bareness of the mountains gave me the feeling that I was back among some of the mountains of southern Spain; such as you will travel along for days, if you ride a mule across Andalusia south of the Sierra Nevada. Djhon-hote went down to the rut of the stream and brought back a few bits of fire-wood; and as I saw that he was anxious to demonstrate his skill before the others, I let him cook all that remained of our sheep; which he did to perfection. We passed the meat from one to the other, taking hold of a good bite with our teeth, then cutting it loose from the rest in true Elizabethan fashion. During this another contingent showed up, Turco-Tartars, and camped alongside us with their animals. Djhon-hote went over to them and exchanged the gossip of the valleys and his latest news from Khassaut. It is obligatory to do this with one's own or the other tribes which live in your region; but a proud Karachaite would not even turn his head for a Suanetian.

Djhon-hote, knowing that we would be travelling for the next day or so in company with large flocks of sheep, wanted to cook a whole one. "Dear one," he said to me, "I will make *shaslik*!" He put his finger-tips to his mouth and kissed them. "I will cut a big forked stick of birch—I will smear it (the side of sheep) with sour cream. . . ." And then he told me how he would roast the meat, finally; one chunk of meat and one chunk of fat (it was better, he said, to do it on a bayonet). "And then we will sit here, each with his stick of *shaslik*—and Dedushka will have a bottle of wine!" I saw no wine in the offing, but we did buy a sheep. Then, like all chefs who want some ingredient that they know is quite unobtainable, he said that to make a perfect *shaslik* we should have some garlic.

The new outfit of Turco-Tartars, with their flat black hats and black side-burns, added to the Spanish colour of the scene. There was a tremendous dignity in their dress and manners. They were beautifully built men, and they made the most of it. Their wasp-waisted *tcherkasskas* showed up their straight backs and square shoulders. Their silvered narrow belts and engraved scabbards gave an *élan* to their presence. Even the most ragged Karachaite, with only one donkey, has a breast covered with cartridge stalls. One of their elders lay beside me, stretched out on a slope of buttercups, and behind him rose a peak of the Caucasus with the clouds already settling on it. His face looked as if it had been hacked out of old teak; and looking at his heavy grizzled old jaw, I felt that he could bite through a bone like any hyena. He sat up to take a cigarette, touched the back of my hand in thanks; and talking with him I suddenly saw what it was that gave these mountain Mohammedans such a queer look about the eyes: the lower lid is absolutely horizontal.

The valley we entered early the next morning, with its pine forests and snow-tipped mountains in the gap ahead of us, might easily have been in the Canadian Rockies; there was the same untamed freshness, the same colouring of rock and trees—and yet, as I have said, there was always the feeling of, for want of a better description, the dust of Asia over it all. We soon left it, however, and started for a saddle whose peaks were 10,000 feet high. This would let us down into Utsch-Kalan, the Karachaite capital.

We climbed through a bare notch and came into a valley where two bands of Karachaites had stopped for a rest. One batch went on down the mountainside of this same valley in search of fresh grass. The other batch joined on to us. A baby boy, of about three, was strapped in the saddle of his father's horse—crying sadly, as the heavy-laden beasts rocked and swayed down the trail. No wonder these Karachaites are some of the best horsemen in the world—when they begin as young as this. The others, including the old ancient with his mule, struck in with us into the deep forest of pines. The great trunks rose around us. The path was strewn with their cones. The old, dead trees shone silver-grey. Golden azaleas covered the floor of this silent forest, and between the gaps in the pines we could see out through great depths of green valleys to the snow crests of the Main Range.

With this lost arm of the Nogai Tartars the scene in the forest was like riding with Genghis Khan; with the Tartars of the Golden Horde advancing on Russia. There was really very little change in the shaven-headed Tartars themselves; their manners and clothes, their silvered daggers—and their wooden bowls and instruments might have been the same as a thousand years ago. These slant-eyed men drove great bulls before them; little donkeys staggered along under goat-skins of sour milk. The trail up through the trees was so steep that we had to get off and walk, almost crawl. The hoofs of the countless animals that had passed this way in the years had bared the roots of the pine trees so that they made webs under our feet. Always, looking back, we could see the valleys of the Caucasus. A cuckoo called before me. . . .

I rode alone. The forest suddenly stopped at a dead, silvered giant. I crossed a bare ridge—and there before me lay a great bowl rimmed by mountain peaks. Its floor was flat. Horses galloped free across it. Great herds of long-horned cattle sent up their cry. Men in broad-brimmed black felt hats were rounding them up. I could hear their yells and the crack of their whips. At the far end, at the edge of dark wall of pine forest, lay a cluster of log cabins. Blue smoke from the evening fires was drifting across the green bowl. Knots of children were romping and playing games outside the log cabins. And at the foot of the cabins lay a small mountain lake. It was, with one exception, the only patch of still water I was to see in all the Caucasus.

I rode down into this peaceful scene. The bowl was like a deep saucer whose edge had broken off short, ending in an abrupt, steep cliff that looked out and down on a long panorama of the Caucasus. There they stretched, blue and green, darkening with the night, with only their highest ridges catching the flames of the sunset. The bowl was full of cattle, sheep, goats, and horses running free. My horse gave an excited whinny as he smelt the strange mares. Kolya was still a stallion. And he was probably bored with Marusha. It seemed to me, as I dismounted, that I heard the sounds of half a hundred udders being milked. The men who had clustered in a group to meet me were entirely different from any other tribesmen I had seen in the Caucasus. Big, heavy-handed men, with blue eyes, they made me remember that in some pockets of the Caucasus there are still the descendants, a bit diluted no doubt, of the original Vikings who had founded Kiev, then rowed on down the Dnieper, crossed the Black Sea, and finally settled in these mountains. It is more than probable that here were some of them. They picked up our bags as we unsaddled and carried them into what appeared to be their best cabin, where a noble-faced young man, who had been hastily arranging a floor-bed of fresh straw, smilingly invited Wicksteed and myself to sit on the smooth log which made one side of it. A bustling old Babushka and a bashful young girl in pink bloomers timidly produced the usual bowl of sour cream, maize bread, and cheese-like butter. This being a ceremony, like the breaking of bread and taking of salt, Wicker and I ate it all.

Outside, the Caucasus were still flaming. The evening's work was in full swing. The cows, after being milked, rushed off at a signal to feed again. Djhon-hote was talking with the men of the settlement, all leaning against the calf-corral. This was an astonishing structure, made from entire lengths of trees, some with the roots still on, and must have been over a hundred feet square. The little donkeys were put inside this with the calves. The goats and sheep were being collected and guided into other enclosures. A boy came past our cabin holding a fresh-born lamb by its front legs. Its mother was running after it, dabbing at it with her nose. Full-grown cattle were allowed to wander freely. And for one of the few times in their lives perhaps Kolya and Marusha were turned out to graze unhobbled. Lights glowed from all the cabin doors.

Uncorrupted by any town, these mountaineers had a strong and assured simplicity. The young man told me that, "before all this happened," they only came up here for the three months' summer grazing. "And now?" I asked, struck by his manner. "God knows," he smiled, and suggested we go for a walk. Outside, he told me that

· 114 ·

his name was Ismail Gluov—and asked me had I ever read Lermontov. "Well," he said, when I told him I had, "I've got a copy of his poems under the straw of my bed—that bed you were sitting on." He then told me that his one desire was to travel; he wanted to see America—"But that is only a dream," he said, laughing suddenly. "I am a fool." (See photo facing p. 16.)

When I asked him how it came that he spoke such good Russian, or so it seemed to me, he laughed again. But a bit grimly this time. "I was a schoolteacher. But they said my father was a *kulak*—because he owned so many animals. So I lost my job and had to come up here. I am very lonely."

He said that if they could possibly manage it, the other men here—there were sixteen families in the settlement—would like to stay here. They did not want to go down into the valleys—"where *they* are!" None of them knew exactly what to do, neither did he; he was now twenty-four, he said. Did I like Pushkin? This strange conversation was carried on as we walked along the log cabins, practically surrounded by corrals. They had two hundred cattle, he said with almost the tone of making a guilty confession, fifty horses, and an uncounted number of goats and sheep. The community also owned a cream-separator, Swedish, that was in the cabin where I would sleep. I could see the fire glowing through each cabin's thick side, as they were made from unshaped tree trunks, without any chinking, originally being intended, as he had just explained, only for summer use. Then I saw that immense fires were burning at all four corners of the settlement. Ismail said that these were "wolf-fires". I thought he was joking; but he said that wolves had taken three sheep only two days before, leaping over the jagged branches that were piled against the outside of every pen. We walked up to one fire, and I saw that it was made of two large trunks, being pushed together as their ends burned. Some small boys, who were standing wolf-guard, proudly stood up to greet us, and Ismail patted one on the head. "Heroes!" he said to me. Then I saw that he was carrying a revolver.

He had grown up beside these same wolf-fires, he told me. Down in his village, he had been delighted with the new school that had come with the Revolution. It was a gate into the open world. It was full of good books. But his father had been classed as a *kulak*; it was true that he owned lots of cattle and did employ other men to

· 115 ·

work for him. So Ismail had been told that he could not continue at the school and one day become a professor. Sons of *kulaks* could not go to school until all the poorer boys had been taken care of. His father, making his peace quickly, or so he thought, with the new régime, had sold off his herds and become a clerk in the local co-operative. But the harm had been done; Ismail was still classed, by the new authorities, as the son of a *kulak*. Ismail had come up here with the few sheep they retained, to watch over them, and to wait in the mountains until they saw what was going to happen. He had not heard from his father. What did I think? That, I told him, would be of no use to him whatever; I knew no more about the future than he did.* And I felt like an impostor that night as old Wicksteed and I, sitting on our bed-log, tried to answer the questions of Ismail and the people who had come in, about Moscow and what life was like there; one awkward reason being that Wicksteed and I did not see at all eye-to-eye about the bliss of life under the Soviets. Wicker always tried to make himself at home with the people, these "friends in the Caucasus"; and I was glad to let him do most of the talking.

The cabin was full of light when I awoke the next morning. The sun was shining through the slits between the logs. It was five o'clock. The Babushka already had the separator going. A young girl stood by it. She must have been about sixteen. She wore, like all these mountain girls, a high-waisted calico dress. But I saw that she had on the Mohammedan trousers underneath. Her figure was slender, but her eyes were broad and blue, with level brows under a delight of golden hair. She was beautiful. The thought came at once: What a pity—that such loveliness should be wasted. Do the men here appreciate such radiance? They seem to treat the women as servants —to fetch and carry, and pour water over their hands. Have you ever had a beautiful girl stand before you, waiting as you wash, to pour water into your cupped hands? It is a delightful sensation, to have a handmaiden. With the pine forests fresh with dew. . . .

Babushka made a cornpone cake. She mixed a round, flat disc with water and corn-meal, slapping it between her two hands. She was seventy years old, old Babushka, and her face was hard and crisp as a nut. She baked the cornpone in an oven of two iron plates placed under the ashes. We had butter for breakfast and fresh cream with our coffee. This place had the spirit of *Evangeline*.

* All the 150,000 Karachaites were deported to Siberia in 1944.

Breaking camp—the morning this poor specimen of a Karachaite tried to leave us in the lurch . . .

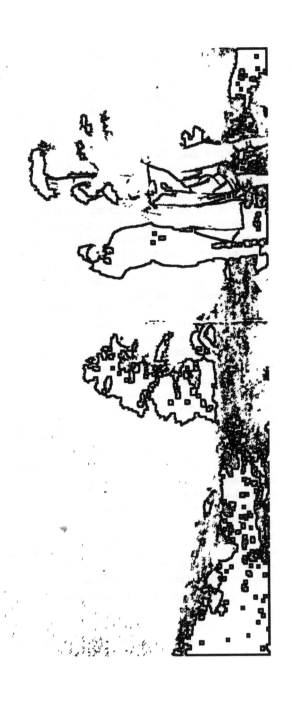

XI

DJHON-HOTE pointed to a bare mountain slope, showing a murky green grass over the red limestone, and said that if it did not rain in the next two days *that* grass would die. This seemed incredible after all the rains we had come through. Yet it helped to understand the Karachaites' life. He said the men of the log cabins had told him that he had better halt this side of Utsch-Kalan and give his horses a good graze. There was no hay in the villages there: last winter's had gone and this year's was not cut yet. And we dared not feed our animals on the lands outside the villages. Their own horses needed that.

We camped that night along a line of *koshes*, about four hours' ride from Utsch-Kalan, so that we could get in there about midday, as Djhon-hote wanted to turn back on the same one. He was in a gloomy mood. And it was not at all in accord with the principles of Western hospitality, mused the ever-quipping Wicksteed (whose heart was gay at the thought that, a few days after Utsch-Kalan, he would be in Teberda, that part of the Caucasus which he really knew, and where he had many friends) for Adami Ezdenov, as our host introduced himself, to offer us his family bed, the best seats by the fire, give us all the sour cream and goat's cheese that we could take—and then try to sting us for the price of a sheep. "But this is the East," announced Wicker, "where Time begins."

"That is why," he said, supping away at his pipe, "you Americans are always in such a damned rush. You *have* no time: these people here have used it up, long before it gets to you."

In this case we decided that if time meant nothing to Adami Ezdenov it should also mean nothing to us. We would hold out as long as he did. He had demanded ten roubles for a sheep; we had offered our usual seven. "No bazaar-bargaining," said Wicker. "Ten is his 'laughing price'; our seven is final."

So we sat there before the *kosh* fire, the only light in this hut of stone and sod. Our host was squatting, watching our faces for any sign of softening. Djhon-hote, who was capable of talking for forty minutes without allowing anyone else to get in a word, was reciting some blood-curdling tale of the hills—or of the Communists—to the other Karachaite shepherds. Wicksteed and I made some tea. We seemed so satisfied with it, occasionally nibbling a rubbery bit of Adami's tasteless cheese, that the old man began to crack. He said if we would wait a moment he would go along the *kosh* and speak to another *khasain* (proprietor). He came back smiling and said that the other proprietor would let us have a sheep for eight roubles. We said seven—and began to make obvious preparations for going to bed.

"Eight is cheap," said Djhon-hote, his mouth watering for some mutton. "In the bazaar, Utsch-Kalan, you will have to pay ten. Eight is a bargain."

"Seven," said Wicksteed.

I felt much like Djhon-hote. The distance was close. Yet this seemed a bargaining cul-de-sac from which neither side could back out. Adami seemed adamant. And in all seriousness Wicksteed and I began to arrange our pile of straw, feeling a little gaunt over the thought of the crisp mutton we might have eaten. Just as we began to undress, Adami suddenly thought of another *khasain*. He rushed out in the night and stayed there ten minutes . . . and when he returned, we had miraculously obtained a sheep for seven roubles. The other *khasain*, said Adami, had just returned to the *kosh*. A palpable ruse to save his face.

He brought the lamb to the fire and showed it to us. All right? As it seemed identical with the first lamb we had been shown (and probably was it), we nodded. The *khasain* took a whetstone and sharpened his fluted dagger. "Good Lord!" gasped Wicker, "he's going to kill it right here!" But then Adami took the live lamb and the knife and went outside. In some ten minutes it was being roasted while our host was busy cutting out some of the choicest bits.

During this operation we were served with a strange cooked cheese, filled with butter, over which was a maizebread crust. Sweet-sour, gummy, but stuff that made you want to eat on and on. It was cooked between the usual two iron pans, placed together in the embers. We ate it by breaking off a piece of crust and scooping out the rest of it with our crust and fingers. Daggers loosened up the bits that stuck to the bottom.

Adami took a huge iron pot and hung it on the chain that dangled from the sod roof over the fire—all this, mind you, in a squatting, even crawling, position; for in these *koshes* it is impossible to stand upright—and he began to throw in chunks of sheep. He chopped it up on the wood block on which he had just been sitting. He did it with an axe, wiping it on his boot after each stroke. He washed the toasted forelegs and threw them, skin and all, into the boiling cauldron. The girls in their flowered bloomers helped in this ritual; and I saw that they had little silver rings on their forefingers and crescents of gold for ear-rings. One of them, with arched eyebrows and a face as oval as an almond, poured water from a long-necked copper urn over Adami's hands. Her eyes were monstrous, grey-green. A lovely little thing. But in a few years she would be as worn as the old hag by the fire. Better for her if, like the Cossack girls, she had a good time before she married, when they are extremely free in their relations with men. These Mohammedan girls are not allowed such liberty.

When the big black pot boiled, and the bubbling foam rose, Adami scraped off the dirty discoloured suds with a stick. He swept it off into the ever-cleansing fire. The sheep for the *kosh* was cooking. . . . The men began to smile and roll cigarettes. The women, in the shadows, formed a little bed of white-turbanned heads. They began to sing. Strange, hesitant little song, carried on the thread of that high, whining cry from the East; and the men seemed to carry the setting of it, humming in different keys. The women sat under suspended saddles and silvered bridles. Adami took his sharp stick and prodded the bits of lamb. More wood . . . more salt. . . . The flames lighted up the soot-blackened stones and the sticky roof. We lay stretched out on our bed of straw. Soon there would be hot meat for all. The song ceased.

Adami took off the pot. The steaming bits of sheep were placed on a split log. They took them in their fingers, blew on them, and tore at the bones with their teeth. Our host insisted that they did not want to eat alone. Our hands and faces were greasy. The slender girl crouched before us, the copper urn in her silvered-ringed hand pouring out a small trickle into our cupped hands. We washed as best we could, merely distributing the grease. Djhon-hote spread out his saddle-cloths and used his saddle for a pillow. I took off my shoes and crawled into my flea-bag; and as I lay there, lazily smoking, I heard the old women eating what sheep there was left.

*　　*　　*

The next morning we climbed out of a valley of tall pines and came out on a spur overlooking Utsch-Kalan. It was one of the most spectacular scenes I had seen anywhere in the Caucasus. Against a far skyline of snow mountains, belted with dark forests, two rivers were racing below us—to meet and form the Kuban river that flowed to the Sea of Azov. The smaller, pouring down from the glaciers of Mt. Elbruz, was glacial grey: there are eighty-four square miles of glaciers around the two peaks of Elbruz. The other, a vivid peacock-green, was the headwater of the Kuban itself. These two rivers met— and then flowed along, like a sharply marked two-coloured ribbon, before they were churned into one in the bronze gorge about a mile farther down. The mist of some rapids rose from the gorge and we could faintly hear its low roar. It was difficult to believe that these fierce rivers from thereon became the broad Kuban, flowing richly through the Northern Caucasus, on its 500-mile flow to the Azov and Black Seas. Utsch-Kalan, which itself lies at 4,500 feet, was nearly three thousand feet below us. We could see people and animals moving; but instead of the collected houses I had expected to meet, we saw just a long straggle of wooden settlements stretched out along the two rivers. While we were standing there looking down on all this we were joined by a toothless old *hadji*, who rode out of the woods behind us. He was mounted on a beautiful chestnut horse and had a white turban bound round his red fez. He also seemed impressed. We stood there in silence, each with his own thoughts, looking down on the capital of Karachay. All of these people have gone now; deported to the wastes of Siberia. . . .

XII

I TAKE this from my notebook, just as most of this book is transposed from notes written by the light of campfires in the Caucasus. If, in the light of later events, it may seem a naïve appreciation of the Communists, it at least has the veracity of being true to the time: no one, not even the leaders, could have foreseen the way that the Kremlin, perhaps as an inevitable outcome of the police state, would abolish all liberties in the name of liberty. After a few days in Utsch-Kalan, I wrote:

"When it comes to dealing with the inherent stupidity, the greed, and the shiftlessness of the average Russian peasant, I am on the side of the Communists. They are at least trying to show him the way to a better life; and if the peasant resists—like the stupid cow which just won't believe it is being led to a better pasture—and the Communists appear brutal in their methods of forcing him, their intentions are unquestionably honest. If they are going to have the last word in this struggle, the peasant is going to progress—and it is refreshing to see what a handful of Russians are doing in Utsch-Kalan."

Here is the way fellow-travellers are made; for although those Russian instructors we met in the Karachaite capital, most of them from Moscow, were almost unbearably arrogant, even infuriating with their assumption of having the answers to everything, they were all inspired by their cause. And this inspired anyone who watched them at work. I have not the least doubt, even now, that the lower ranks of these Communists in the Caucasus, the "workers in the field," all believed that they were leading the mountaineers to a new and glorious life; a communal existence in which each person worked for the good of all, and in which—here is where the naïvety came in—human nature was going to be reformed and all greed would vanish. Over at Kislovodsk we had taken a dislike to the Communists we encountered; but they, as I have written, struck us

as being the exploiters of Communist privileges; slick, party poli-
ticians who were enjoying the plums of the régime: a state-paid
holiday of three or four weeks at the most favourite of all the
Caucasian spas. Here in Utsch-Kalan, despite the wild beauty of its
setting, there were no such "pickings"; the Communists stationed
there regarded it as exile; and I found myself envying their idealism.

Utsch-Kalan was then a region of scattered board settlements,
some 1,200 homes in all, strung out in little hamlets—each with its
own wooden mosque—along the bare valleys of these two rivers.
A few of what were, supposedly, the best of these houses had tin
roofs; and they nearly all had square wooden chimneys, plated
with tin—rusty tin. It was a tawdry scene. It took us a day or
so to realise that the green fields we saw coming in held about
all the grass there was in this region; and that if they did not get
rain in a few days even that would die. These particular Karachaites
had been driven into these unfertile valleys in the days of the
Tsars, when their rich mountain grazing lands had been turned
over to the Cossacks; those inexorably advancing Cossacks of the
Line, soldier-settlers, with whom the Russians finally conquered all
the wild Caucasus. Penned in here, having constantly to knuckle-
under, barely able to get a living from their hostile and over-grazed
soil, these particular Karachaite tribesmen had lost their mountain
characteristics, the boldness and ready good-humour of the types
we had just come through; and our first impressions of them were
that they were a rather cunning and debased lot. This may have
come, of course, from the fact that Utsch-Kalan was really the first
place in the Caucasus where we were thrown in close contact with
the Russian instructors, and that we looked at the local tribesmen
through Russian eyes. This is self-evident from my notes; for as you
have seen, I spoke of the Karachaites here as "peasants"; and that
is just about the last name one would think of applying to a
Caucasian mountaineer, sitting so proudly on his horse in the midst
of his wild scenery, where he is the very picture of freedom. The
Russians, probably to get away from the old associations, were
building another capital for the Karachaites, at the junction of the
Kuban and Teberda rivers: pride-arousing stone buildings, to replace
the warrens of wooden huts. A modern community town with
massive Mt. Elbruz as the back-drop. A magnificent site, with a
motor-bus road then being cut through to the distant railroad. But

that model capital would not be ready for years to come: to the Karachaites the old wooden buildings strung out along the rivers, the trading stores and wine-shops, and the rock-studded dirt streets were the very apex of civilisation, hub of their world.

We could readily understand that, for we had come to this settlement like any mountaineer, riding through lonely mountains and deep forests; to where, thousands of feet below, we saw the sudden sight of hundreds of wooden houses lying along the grey-green and peacock-blue rivers; racing to merge in the big bronze gorge below. Rivers literally leaping from rock to rock to escape from their prison in the Caucasus. We rested there looking down on the rivers and the people moving below us. I felt as I sat on my horse in the bright sun, experiencing such varied emotions, that here was another scene that I had better let go by default; decide not to write it. For if it is true that most of the best things of travel are those that you have not set out to get, so it is that the best stories you bring back are those you never attempt to tell. They are too much for you. Wicksteed must have felt much of the same bewilderment, this spell of the Caucasus; for, leaning against my horse, he stared down as if stupefied—a silence which I finally broke by saying lightly: "Well, Wicker— there's our trout!"—for I knew that if I did not get some trout out of *that* gorge, I would get none in the Caucasus. I got seven that night, one close to a pound. And a few days later, fishing the head-waters of the Kuban, I got thirty-five; the largest number of trout I have ever caught in one day, or wanted to catch. But, as you will see later, it was a day with a tragic finish.

The old mullah also seemed silenced by the beauty of this scene, and just shook his head wonderingly as we turned our horses to find the trail down. Zigzagging slowly, we left the pines and finally got down to a good road, riding past quivering aspens and tall poplars that stood like sentinels by the stream; and then, rounding the toe of the spur, blazing in the sunlight, we saw the snows of Mt. Elbruz. We entered a grassy valley where the grey river raced through fields of green splashed with large sweeps of yellow globe-flowers. On a gravelled stretch of open bank, we saw hundreds of horsemen, and rode among them. Swarthy, untamed-looking men, all dressed in the wasp-waisted Circassian *tcherkasskas*, soft glove-like boots, each man carrying the beautiful fluted Caucasian dagger. As fine a set of horsemen as I have ever looked at, and even their splendid little horses seemed to share their pride. All these men were in black, with wide-brimmed black hats or arrogant headpieces of black lamb's wool. The women were like a flower bed; in dresses of turquoise, peacock-green, yellow, and scarlet. This was Fair Day; and the Karachaites had been coming in from the surrounding mountains dressed in all their finery.

Here was a civilisation all of its own: nearby valley farmers coming in in their grotesque lumbering ox-carts, immense two-wheelers, with wicker bodies on them as long as whale-boats; the springless, yet unbreakable, little *lineakas*, the rattling four-wheeler that had almost broken my spine over at Kislovodsk; horsemen who had come down from the remotest settlements; and a handicraft of black, soft-pummelled Caucasian saddles; black felt *burkas*, home-made sombreros; felt rugs; wooden spoons; bowls of copper and brass; displays of eggs, cheese, sour cream, soap, salt; bolts of cloth; beautiful daggers from Daghestan; horses. And as a Caucasian loves his horse even more than his wife, the horse-traders were the focus of male interest in the Utsch-Kalan bazaar.

The little cluster of white-painted houses which marked the beginning of the new capital had not a room to spare, and Wicker and I were given a place to sleep on the floor of the new school house. Putting on a fresh jacket of Harris tweed, which I had brought back from London and not yet worn in Russia, I pushed my arm into its sleeve—and pushed out a pair of silk stockings! I had smuggled them in that way for my secretary. But now, as they fell right at the feet of the young schoolmistress, who had come in to get my laundry, I (what would you do, chum?) surrendered them. She was ecstatic. She was a tiger-blonde Cossack, and she wasted no time in useless conventions. Her own pretty legs were bare and brown as a nut. She sat down on the floor and pulled on those lovely silk stockings, right there and then, before me; then the colour flushed into her face, she gave a laugh and ran out: in pulling on the stockings she had reached the point where we both came to the same thought—she had no garters. That broke the ice at Utsch-Kalan.

Wicker and I, with our green canvas bucket, went shopping and laid in a good supply of eggs. We found, to our dismay, that that was about all we could buy; though in the local co-operative we lingered and watched the price of many a good sheep being exchanged for bolts of printed cotton. I saw more goods here, in

The glacial valley leading up to the Klukhor

proportion to its size, than I saw in the huge Mostorg in Moscow. Among them was an exhibition of prize atrocities: some hideous brass-bound trunks, with brass filigree, which, we were told proudly, had been made in Nijni-Novgorod. We were quickly taken in charge and led to a clean dispensary, where we were shown babies and adults being examined free of charge, medicines given without payment, and where people considered to be seriously ill were being urged to remain for treatment, or perhaps an operation—most of whom looked already half scared to death. Obeying the code of a distinguished visitor being shown the sights, I asked questions, showed an interest (which was not hard to do), and even went so far as to pat the back of a spotted baby. When I asked what was wrong with it, I got the reply:

"Smallpox."

I kept my hands to myself after that although I had just been vaccinated, and inoculated against almost every form of known disease, before leaving London. I doubt if the child had it; it was probably said out of eagerness to impress us with the seriousness of their mission. We were chased about during the next days on various tours of inspection, and tired quickly after having had such peace in the mountains. Wicksteed and I made ourselves at home on the schoolroom floor, got out our books, and lay down to enjoy ourselves on our bed-rolls. There was a cold nip in the air, and the gay little Cossack schoolmistress kept a fire going in the *petchka*, the tall porcelain clay stove; in which, opening its door, Wicker and I fried ourselves a dozen eggs. "Beauty is an unsettling thing, isn't it?" mused Wicker, as the schoolmistress stood there watching us. "Look at that girl's breasts!" It was hard not to.

She had placed herself in charge of us. There had been a male teacher, she informed us, from Rostov-on-Don; but he had gone off for the summer, taking his bed with him. Which, I gathered, implied that he did not intend to come back. Here, on the clean school floor, we experienced all the sensations of being two animals on exhibit. One after another—and there were forty-eight of them—all the members of the Russian colony, these instructors in Communism, came in to look at us, to satisfy their curiosity. These, we knew quite well, included several members of the G.P.U., though we never knew which. The most frequent—and obstreperous—was a burly young Don Cossack, dressed in spotless white, who, for reasons I could not discover—probably just simple good-heartedness—seemed to have taken a fancy to us. It took me a couple of days to decide whether I was going to like him or hate him: he was around us like a fly. Although the President of the Utsch-Kalan Soviet was a Karachaite, his assistant was a Russian: a quiet, pale-faced, determined-looking young man, who, it did not take long to see, was boss of the whole show. He came in with the policeman, when we were asked for our passports; and he was not in the least friendly. Wicker and I knew the type. We saw that in all the offices, such as the Ispolkom, the local Karachaites were being allowed to hold the signs of office—but the forty-eight "instructors in civilisation and government," as the young Don Cossack proudly spoke of himself and his comrades, were doing the real work. This seemed to suit the local Karachaites right down to the ground: they had the token of power—and no responsibility.

In spite of their irritating complacency and their cocksureness that everything they were putting in was going to take root and grow, in that brave new world they were building, it was impossible not to admire these eager young Russians; turning their hands to schooling, doctoring, government, sanitation (which last, at least, I felt would remain theoretical). But the most impressive figure I met in Utsch-Kalan was an old country doctor, who had been there forty years. No one but the young Cossack girl seemed to attach any importance to him, but she obviously thought he was the finest Russian of them all, a feeling with which I fully agreed. He was a delightful old chap, a relic of the old régime, who had come down to the Caucasus in Tsarist days "to see what I could do here." Now he was caught in the new medical scheme, a servant of Moscow; but that made no difference, he smilingly told us. "I love the Caucasus, I love the people, and—I love my work. I have never made any money anyway, so what is the difference? I love my work, therefore I am happy."

The diseases of dirt were by far the most prevalent, he told us. And then, the constant diet of maize-meal, which these lower mountaineers lived upon almost exclusively, gave them a wide range of abdominal complaints. But he could see no alternative—"These are very, very poor people". He gave us tea, talked about Chekov, whose stories he apparently knew by heart—"You see, I do not get many books, down here in the Caucasus. . . ." And as we walked away, and

I told the Cossack girl that I had found him "very sympathetic", she squeezed my arm in gratitude. It was restoring to meet such a contented and useful man; I only hope they let him be.

Life here was exile for most of the young Russians. They laughed derisively when I spoke of the beauty of the Caucasus. "You just try living here! Try that! You'll soon get enough of it." Yet when I was drinking a bottle of Naperiouli, that potent purple wine of the Caucasus, in the local grog-shop at sunset, one came in and seizing my arm pulled me outside—"Look!" I could not at first see what he was so excited about; then I realized that I was staring at one of the most beautiful things I had ever seen. The immense cone of Mt. Elbruz, which seemed to have moved in so that it towered all over us, was slowly, silently turning faint rose in the sunset. And that night the obstreperous Don Cossack came along, also asked me to come outside, and suggested that we go down to the little wooden bridge crossing the river. There I found a cluster of Russians, who emptied my case of Gold Flakes; and in silence we watched the moon rise over the Caucasus. The new moon. I had seen the last of the old one at Kislovodsk. I mentioned this, saying that I would be off in a day or so, up the Teberda valley; and it would be pleasant to have that moon, as I was going to try to get over the Klukhor Pass and down to Sukhuum on the Black Sea.

"Lucky fellow!" they said enviously. "You'll soon be back in Moscow."

*   *   *

A footnote to history may be added here: the Karachaites (population 150,000) sided with the Germans during the German drive into the Caucasus, in 1942, in the Second World War. As a result their autonomous semi-republic was abolished, Georgia being given the major part of it; its population was deported to Siberia in 1944—along with the entire Tchetchen, Balkar and Inguish tribes—and Utsch-Kalan (which under its Republic had been named after a member of the Politburo: Mikoyan-Shakar) is now called Klukhori, and belongs to the Georgian S.S.R.   Another gift from Stalin to his own people; who, with these other fanatically freedom-loving tribesmen deported, have now become the master people of the Caucasus.

XIII

ON my first afternoon at Utsch-Kalan I managed to slip away
from the crowd, took my rod, and went down to the bronze
gorge where the two rivers were merged in rapids. It was slow and
difficult work to fish this water. I got seven trout; the first being such
a surprise that I could not believe I had him on. This was the best
fish of the seven that I got. Luckily I reached a spot in the gorge,
just at sunset, where I could not go any farther; so I had time to
get out into open country before the night came down. Wicker was
sitting disconsolately, waiting for me—"I was beginning to wonder
whether you had managed to fall in and drown yourself!" I laid the
trout on the floor. The speed with which he got the frying pan and
put fresh kindling into the fire of the *petchka* said more than words
how he appreciated my luck. I cleaned them, and we smoked for a
while, to let the kindling become embers; then we put a couple of
big pats of butter into the pan, watched it sizzle, and placed all the
seven trout in it at once. I had only one large one, which, indeed,
must have been close to a pound. "And now for a quick swim!"
exulted Wicker. "So that we will feel properly fresh for them."
Would you believe it, we forgot the trout! We had hung on to rocks
in the racing Kuban, letting the delightful water riffle over us; then
we had sat there smoking. "My God—*the trout!*" he suddenly yelled,
and dashed back, as naked as an Indian.

But the trout were safe. We took them out, and they were done to
a turn. A wee bit crisp perhaps; but I like them that way. The little
Cossack schoolmistress came in while we were eating, and I showed
her the backbone of the biggest trout. She dashed out to fetch the
obstreperous young Don Cossack Instructor in Communism. He
asked me how I had caught them, and I showed him my fly-book.
"Ha!" he cried—and I am sure these were the first flies he had ever
seen—"Our man here has caught fish twice as big as *that*," pointing
to the backbone. "But he knows how—*he* uses worms." By that

time I was beginning to loathe the man. He was alienating the admiration of our little Cossack girl. *"You wait!"* I told him, grimly.

Here time was on my side. Djhon-hote left us at Utsch-Kalan, striking back that same day with the faithful Kolya and Marusha: much as he loved us, he tried to explain, he knew nothing whatever of the country beyond, and nothing was going to make him go in there. We had to wait at Utsch-Kalan until we could find a man with two horses who knew the trails and would go over with us. No one about the school knew of any horses that we could hire. Wicksteed and I suspected that it was probably the Russians in the district, the police, being deliberately unhelpful. They had probably set some story going that had made the local Karachaites suspicious of us. After a few futile days, we decided to try for horses in the little settlements far up the Kuban river. The Russians had told us there was a fine Narzan spring up there, big enough to bathe in, and using that as a pretext, we hired a *lineaka* and set off. I took my rod along.

I thought I might have a try at some bits of quiet water farther up. The river looked so enticing that I took my share of the bread and cheese and let Wicker go on to have his exciting Narzan bath, and try to find a new pair of horses. I sat down on the bank of the Kuban to enjoy the scenery. This was on the edge of an open, swift stretch of river, where it was racing down in a succession of step-like rapids. I watched the clouds begin to come to anchor on the mountain peaks. It began to cloud over. I took out my slab of bread and cheese and began my lunch. I had put a 3X cast in to soak before I began this; and now I put on a little orange-and-green fly, a "United Ireland," that I had bought over in Connemara a few years before. It was just the first one that came handy. And with this, and the sandwich in my left hand, I was idly whipping the water, when—*wham!* I had a trout. In my excitement I dropped the bread and cheese into the swift river. The trout was a little beauty. It was about seven inches long, light moss-green on the back, with vivid scarlet spots. I had a cast with two points, and I quickly put on a Peter Ross and a Zulu. A few casts, and I had another trout; exactly the same size, and again on the "United Ireland." Then another. It was amazing, the speed with which they shot for a rock or a bit of sunken tree, to foul me

All these trout were firm and fat, light green on the back, like the colour of the water, all with these vivid red spots. I laid them on the grass beside me. It was only after the *lineaka* had long since been gone that I realized I had left my bag in it, with Wicksteed's lunch and the bottle of Naperiouli. As I needed my net to land the fish, I wet some grass to cover these and went on with my fishing. The river flowed in some lovely pools between the white stretches of broken water; and here and there, where a pine had fallen, long pools had been made, nearly every one of which had a sandy bank. I saw one such deep and long pool below me, and putting my trout back in the net I pushed my way through the pine woods down to its foot. I took fourteen trout out of that pool. The brush was thick here; sufficient reason, no doubt, with all the insects dropping in from the overhanging bushes, for the trout's quick rise to the fly. I was using three "United Irelands" now, having said to myself: "If they seem to prefer these, then these are what I shall present to them."

It was the only time in my life that I have ever had three trout on at the same time, which happened twice that day. I had no idea how to land them: I just took a chance, hauled the top fish on shore, put the net under the tail fish, and scooped in the in-betweener. A fish-hog?—not a bit of it: I was thinking of that obstreperous young Don Cossack, the Instructor of Communism. And of old Wicksteed. Wicksteed, who had fished in Norway, or been with people fishing there; and who, probably having forgotten it, cried out when I got back to Utsch-Kalan that night: "Ye Gods! I am a poor man—I have never yet been able to have all the trout that I could eat at one sitting—but tonight is the night!" (He had, of course, been unable to find me, fishing down by the river, as he came back with the *lineaka*.)

I went mad. When I saw trout rise up through that aquamarine world to strike . . . ! Well, I could watch their whole battle. I was trembling with delight. With the possible exception of one or two, none of these trout was up to half a pound. Three to a pound would have been the right estimate. And they were quite sophisticated. I have never known it answered yet: whether trout who have never been fished over are much more stupid than others. I know that if I walked up brazenly to a pool, I saw them shoot down. They took just as much catching, it seemed to me, as ordinary brook trout. Of course, I am not comparing the trout of the Kuban to those of rivers where there are more rods than fish. When they rushed, boring for the white water or for any obstruction, they telegraphed their struggle through the line: I had to tire them out, net the lower fish first—for

I had plenty of doubles. And it was all unexpected; as good a day's fishing as I have had anywhere in my life.

I did not know how tired I was until I sat down to count them, and found that I had twenty-one. I was sitting there quietly, looking up at the mountains, when an eagle soared out from them, circled slowly, and then, throwing up his mighty pinions, dropped with a jerk on the bank right opposite me. I was watching him, wondering what he was about to do; when, suddenly, with fright written all over him, he simply scrambled into the air. I heard a noise, turned, and saw three shaggy Circassians riding down to the bank.

They saw with amazement the long line of shining trout that I had spread out to count. They stared at my rod. They did not know what to make of it; so light and flexible—like a whip! It occurred to me that they had never seen a fly, so I showed them the bright feathers and the green-and-orange body—and then, with a little nick, I pulled the sharp hook against one of their tough thumbs. The man jumped in surprise, yanked his hand back; and the others laughed at him. With gestures, they asked could they watch me catch some fish. I nodded and they tethered their horses. I gave one of them the heavy net, full of fish, and we dumped them out at the foot of a likely stretch of river down below. The sight of a trout fighting was almost more than they could stand; they wanted to help me—rush in and pull it out, like children. They came along with me, and I got thirteen fish out of the mile of river going up. Then, as the sun was beginning to sink, their interest began to wane. They each solemnly shook hands with me, then smiled to show how much they had enjoyed themselves, and walked off shaking their heads. I caught one more fish, and then got out on the dirt road just as darkness came down.

I have seldom been so dead beat as I was that night when I finally reached Utsch-Kalan. My left foot, in the felt surgical boot, seemed to weigh a ton; and no wonder, for I had waded in it, regardlessly half a dozen times that day. But triumph was mine. I stopped in the grog shop to buy two bottles of Naperiouli. The Don Cossack, as I had hoped, was in there. God had delivered him into my hands. . . .

"Now!" I said, making squiggly motions with my fingers, "what about worms?"

I invited him to come back to dinner, and gave him the net to carry—just so he would properly appreciate the weight of it. I might say that I had dumped the whole thirty-five out on the wineshop's floor, making everyone in there take a look and properly admire them; and the Don Cossack, noble fellow, had actually slapped me on the back and called me an *"Ochen kheetri chelovek!"*—a "Clever one!" Just the admission that I wanted from him. I began to like him immensely.

It was impossible, of course, to cook all those trout in the clay stove. I gave them to the little Cossack schoolmistress to cook, and invited her to the big dinner. "I'll show her how!" laughed the Don Cossack, as Wicker and I went down to the river for a cold dip. Wicker told me that he had got the two horses; they would be outside the school the next morning. "And now," he spluttered, as he squeezed the cold water from his beard—"now for the dinner of a lifetime!"

Well . . .

I can hardly bear to write this. We were all four sitting at table. Wicker, being the eldest, we had unanimously made Master of Ceremonies. This by placing a large platter of friend trout before him. He put three or four on each plate and handed them to us. The Cossack girl took a munch, and said something in Russian that sounded like—Yum-yum! The Instructor in Communism just tilted back his head and dropped a whole trout down his gullet. Wicksteed, fastidiously splitting a trout to remove its backbone, then took a large bite. He choked, hastily put his handkerchief before his mouth. "My God!" he gasped. "What *is* it?"

Well—they had cooked the trout in sunflower-seed oil. But not only that; they had *soaked* them in cold oil first. This I discovered when I rushed out into the kitchen to save what might be left of them. There they all lay in that disgusting fluid. *"Nu vot!"* said the Instructor in Communism, who had followed us. "That's the way they cook them in *my* village!"

I would rather have eaten cotton-waste soaked in engine oil. I went back to the table and lighted a cigarette. No, I told the little Cossack girl, I did not feel hungry: perhaps I was a little too tired. . . . Never hearing or even noticing Wicksteed's stunned silence, she and that damned Cossack merrily ate the rest of the trout.

We have crossed the glacial lake and think we are on the last lap of the Klukhor

XIV

THERE was only one occasion in our wanderings among the mountain shepherds of the Caucasus when we were refused hospitality; and that, I feel sure, was chiefly due to the miserable disposition of our Karachaite guide, whom we picked up at Utsch-Kalan. He was a whining fellow; always moaning about something being wrong with his spine, and worrying about what we might do to his saddle-galled horses.

On this night we had come down to a mountain shelf from a pass which the map said was 9,800 feet high. Maybe it was; there were clouds a-plenty around and below us. And the most amazing thing was that, unlike the Klukhor which had snow as low as 7,000 feet, there was not a flake of snow on this pass. The shelf was as cold as the Arctic. It was the one night, unfortunately, when we would have been willing to sleep under a crude roof no matter how dirty the floor was. But "Spine," as I now called him, put up such a whining show of it to the owners of the log cabin that we lost caste with them. They regarded us suspiciously and left us to make a tent of my ground-sheet as a refuge from the dew-drenched grass.

"Spine" was too stricken by his malady even to collect wood for our fire, much less to roast some lamb on a spit to make us *shaslik*. So I cooked the inevitable rice-and-raisins over a meagre fire. Djhou-hote would have had these Karachaites stepping it, and sour cream to spread over the roasting meat, because he liked such things himself. It was a wrench to have to part with him; but nothing could make him go one foot over this new pass. When the "Spine" groaned and lay down to sleep behind our miniature tent, wrapped in his felt cloak, with his saddle for a pillow, I suspected that he would desert us in the morning.

He did. He was already saddled before we woke up. I made no effort to keep him. But I told him that he was either going to take us and our gear down into the valley, or he was going to get us two more horses. I did not care which. And he stood there, scratching his head and telling us how much his spine hurt (see photo facing p. 112), while Wicker and I got our breakfast and began to strike camp. When he saw that he was not going to get paid until he did one or the other, he glumly disappeared and came back after a time with another man. This shepherd was also ill; *he* complained of "fire in the stomach"—probably the common affliction of worms—and his mare, which I was given to ride, had a four-day-old foal with her. He also brought a wistful little donkey, instead of a horse, for our packs. The mare and foal were an awkward combination that gave me all the sensations of riding a quick-lunch. For the mare, stopping to eat wherever she could, always had the foal running up to her, to nuzzle her for more breakfast, luncheon, or dinner. At other times the beautiful little foal ran just ahead of her mother's legs, always threatening to trip us and send us bouncing down the mountainside.

But our shepherd was either related to, or was a friend of, every other shepherd in the adjacent valleys; and the next night, after a day of ascending and descending mountainsides, much of it above the timber-line and with some grand views of the snowy mountains, we came to another cluster of stone huts, high up in the mist, along the sides of a gorge. Here the owners of the best *kosh* immediately set to to make it ready for us. We bought a whole sheep, and lay by the hearth-fire full to drowsiness with a dinner of mutton roasted on wooden sticks and sweetly garnished with a coating of rich cream. The corncakes in this *kosh* were hot and light. The stone and sod ceiling was so low that one did literally have to crawl to move about inside it (see photo facing p. 80); yet the harness hanging from the central post had heavy silver filigree. And here, squatting by the primitive fire, I met the finest specimen of Karachaite manhood I had ever seen.

He was a superb specimen, a good six feet high, broad and deep-chested, every line and feature of his bronze face those of the ideal Mongol aristocrat. Talking not a word of my tongue, his eyes were quick to grasp the expression on my face, his laugh and white teeth flashed at every chance for humour. And yet, though he was twenty-four years old and the figure of some ancient princeling, he was afraid to take a cigarette from me in front of his father.

Here, in one of the thousand isolated pockets of the Caucasus, we had stumbled on what seemed an absolutely untainted form of the patriarchal existence, the tribe of the Old Man. The teaching of the Communists might have begun to penetrate into the villages far below; the emancipation of women, slow as it was, might have been started down there; but here, overlooking this remote and lovely valley, the women were thought as little of as the animals—even less—and the first son of the leader was as obedient as a child to his Grand Old Man. Allah was still worshipped with absolute fidelity. When Wicker and I shared our wine, one of several bottles of purple Naperiouli we had bought in Utsch-Kalan, with our Karachaite horse-wrangler, wretched "Fire-in-the-Stomach," this splendid young Mohammedan laughingly declined our offer to him. When the sheep was killed it was the father who came to administer the knife-stroke that cut its throat, leaving his son and another retainer to do the ugly work of skinning and disembowelling. These people would not eat a piece of meat from an animal that had not been bled to death. And a pig around such a Mussulman community would probably have resulted in the sudden illness, if not the death, of the man who dared to bring it there.

There was, in fact, something very close to a battle on that mountainside before dawn. A tribe of Karachaites had come over the pass with their herds and flocks in search of grass; and another tribe, as it happened, had come into the valley at the same time and for the same purpose; and they had met on the plateau just above our stone huts.

Now these grazing lands in the mountains have a complicated form of ownership. In a sense of the word they belong to no one at all, but it is the unwritten law (at least it was) that those lands adjacent to a village or settlement are sacred to its own horses and cattle, so much so that a stranger coming to a village is not supposed to graze his own horse even on the outskirts. And the mountain lands are, wherever they are occupied, the hereditary grazing rights of that particular *kosh*.

Therefore it came about that while these two particular bands were getting farther from words and nearer to daggers in their argument, our own princeling—with his Grand Old Man—appeared in their midst and told them both to clear out. . . .

We awoke to the laughter of the young princeling and the triumphant voices of his own clansmen. Our own guide, being the only neutral among them, had been acting as peacemaker. He grinned at us and slapped his Daghestan knife. "I made them shake hands!" he said. But I felt, alas, that poor old whining "Fire-in-the-Stomach" would not have made even a good spectator if a real fight had started.

It was understandable why this valley life was so remote and unspoiled; for above its only entrance was the snowy pass and below that was one of the worst trails I have ever seen. It went down in slippery little surfaces along the sheer sides, and then became merely a series of footholds among the chaos of glacial waste. Rocks so formidable that nothing less than dynamite could have shifted them to make a better trail. They were almost protection enough for the coveted patch of grazing land above. It was wearying, almost agonising work to pull ourselves through, wander around or over them. I trusted the horse much more than my own feet.

But the Karachaite horses, men, sheep, and cattle, to say nothing of the piebald goats, cannot be stopped by anything short of the vertical among the wild mountains in which they are born and die. For the foreigner it was not quite so pleasant. I did not like the habit of the foal always trying to get ahead and walk just in front of its mother's legs. I did not like the solicitude of the mare, always turning its head when we were in a ticklish spot, to see if the foal was safely coming after her. And I wondered what would happen to the little animal's slender, still-gawky legs if it did fall. Whereupon it did.

Although there were several *koshes* ahead of us down the valley, the trail was simply ghastly. An eight-inch-wide footpath along a steep hill-slope; zigzags that had been almost obliterated by rain. In places it had been washed out altogether. Then dizzy slides down a jumble of shale and boulders which the horse always tried to refuse. On one of them the foal slipped and fell fifty feet. I tried to grab its tail as it went over, then had to stand there and watch it drop, with sickening thuds, from rock to rock. Its fragile legs! . . . But it fetched up on a shelf of grass, and aside from trembling and whinnying for its mother, did not seem any the worse, although it was urinating a steady stream from fright. The mare, which I was riding, cried frantically, and came much too near to tumbling down herself. I got off and held on to her. "Fire-in-the-Stomach" scrambled along the hillside like a goat, and took the foal in his arms. He caressed it and talked to it and soothed it as if it had been a child. Old Wicker held the mare back while I slid down to help get the foal up. The only sensible animal of the lot of us was the little donkey—wise and lovable little creature—which needed no one to restrain it, and stood there, its eyes closed, one ear back and one ear pointing forward. Then we went down into deep spinneys of birch, into a forest of dark pines with a clear stream running through it, lingered to drink our fill at a Narzan spring bubbling from some red-stained rock; and there, below us, opened up the garden-like valley of Teberda. We passed a tiny wooden mosque (see photo facing p. 97) which had a pathetically crude wood crescent, and a ladder up a tree for the *muezzin* to climb to call the Faithful to prayer.

Wicker took the lead as we came into Teberda: he had friends here—"those hospitable people in the Caucasus"—and he strode at our head, with his long staff. His white beard had gained the proper patriarchal length by now. I came behind, my weary horse nodding her head with each final step, her little anxious-eyed foal keeping as close to her as possible. Then came the ragged Karachaite guide, also plodding; then that wistful little donkey, one ear cocked forward, one back, its wise little eyes almost closed with fatigue. . . . I did not know whether this cavalcade was like something out of *Don Quixote* or Moses leading the Israelites out of Egypt. For old Wicksteed, he had now reached his PROMISED LAND.

XV

TEBERDA, the little Karachaite village lying in a woody, windless corner of the Sukhuum Military Road, had ambitions at that time of becoming Russia's Switzerland, a Caucasian Davos. I was constantly told by the gaunt health-seekers there that its climate was far finer than any in the Alps. They said this earnestly; too earnestly. Only too obviously some of them were in the last stages of T.B. In Teberda I had no doubts about the rights of these people in the *kurots* to enjoy every bit of comfort and life they could cling on to, in their fleeting mountain paradise. In Teberda I met that erratic, but by then forgotten, little Russian genius, Ginsberg, the sculptor whose statues of children were so sought after by the rich Americans of the early 1900's. He, so he told me, was now doing statues of commissars and notable Communists—"especially the dead ones," he added wrily.

In Teberda I knew that I was going to lose Wicksteed. We put up with the Karachaite family he had summered with two years before. They welcomed him as if he was the greatest man they had ever met (which he probably was); and the "great English Professor from Moscow" settled down to enjoy his distinction. Their son followed him about like a dog. And it was this man, Yusef, one of the youngest and cleverest of the Teberdine mountain guides, that I took up to the pass with me. I also knew I was going to lose Wicker the minute we went out to pick wild strawberries with Ginsberg and an assortment of his cronies. This little picnic, so bubbling with the hopes of all the wonderful life that lay ahead, now seems, because of the way these hopes have been travestied, like something from another world; or at any rate, something that happened in the days of far away and long ago. Ginsberg told me that he was only too pleased with his lot: the Kremlin was giving him a pension of £25 a month, a whole room to himself in one of the rest homes, and a free railway pass that allowed him to take a bus from Teberda to Batalpaschinsk, some sixty miles away, and go to Leningrad and back whenever he wanted to. Our companions on that happy little picnic, a busload of us, were a People's Commissar, a man who stoked the furnace in a Moscow textile mill, and a Soviet writer who was later on to make an international name. It was a frolic.

We had taken several young girls with us, some of the most desperately ill cases, and as one looked at their flushed cheeks, and glittering eyes, and the joy they were getting out of hunting for strawberries or shyly making up little bouquets of wild flowers, one felt that the spirit of the good god Pan was in these wild woods. Here really was a life stripped of man's basic greed and meanness. At any rate, for these sick girls, people of no great importance in party politics, it really was like that—at that place and time.

It was invigorating to see that such a mixed bag seemed so absolutely unconscious of rank. Perhaps the People's Commissar did look, as George Orwell so neatly put it, as if "all animals are equal, but some animals are more equal than others." But this busload did not make a point of its democracy and was completely free from that incessant propaganda which in Moscow so frayed the nerves. I tried to imagine, as we hurtled out into the country, just what was really in the minds of each of them: how great was their faith in the Communist code? On that day, spring of 1929 in the flowered Caucasus, I would have sworn that these happy picnickers did not have the least doubt. But when old Wicksteed tried to get on that tack with Ginsberg, the little sculptor smiled and said he had not come to the Caucasus to talk politics. "Neither have I!" said Wicker huffily, rebuffed. "But I am not afraid to!"

Alexander Wicksteed's *Ten Years in Soviet Moscow*, which he wrote after this trip, was a compendium of conversations with chance Russians, hardly one of them an official. For that reason it was markedly different from the inevitable books turned out by newspaper correspondents; and, while shamelessly naïve in its critical attitude, probably came nearer to what real "life in the street" was like in the Russia of those days. I knew that Ginsberg would not escape him. Wicker saw an Intellectual in the little sculptor, and relishing the picture of himself and the artist having afternoons among the daisies and wild strawberries, talks on a high level, marked him down.

That evening he told me that he would not go any farther than

· 139 ·

Teberda. "I am too old. Yusef says that the Klukhor Pass is filled with snow, anyhow. So is the valley leading up to it. We have had the spring of our lives—you and I!—and now I think I will just find a tree here and laze through the rest of the summer."

I did not blame him. I would have liked nothing better myself. But I had to get back to my desk and start sending out political cables again. And the most interesting way back lay over the historic Klukhor Pass; then down the Military Road; then a boat from Sukhuum, after I had eaten my full share of melons; across the Black Sea to Sebastopol in the Crimea, which is a paradise in the spring. I was almost afraid to see the Crimea again; it would awaken too many memories.

But after a few days in Teberda, staring at the snow mountains at the head of the valley, I lusted to climb them. I got two more horses and set off up the obsolete Sukhuum Military Road, which is 209 miles long, originally built to exterminate the Circassians, and had not been repaired since 1913. I parted company with old Wicker, who stepped out to bid me farewell in pyjamas of red and orange. "Good luck," he waved. "Hope I don't see you again—that'll mean you have been turned back by the snows." I envied him the repose of his old pipe and his lazy summer wandering in little off-jaunts through the hills.

The Klukhor is only supposed to be open for 2½ months of the year. It is not free from snow until August. In the little open-air Narzan booth in Teberda they had told me that an "idiot," a nervous wreck, had passed by in May this year, saying he was going to cross the Klukhor Pass. He left Teberda and had not been heard of since. He was on foot; maybe he got over. Or . . . ? Anyway, if Yusef and I got our horses over, we would be the first this year.

This was enticing but not too encouraging. And the very road up from Teberda seemed to have a mysterious, ill-omened quality to it. To begin with, it heads at once into a deep pine forest. A dark trail— with strange holes in the bank from which come gusts of ice-cold air. The breath of the mountains. The Ganatchkir, a glacier river, thunders down this dark valley and is the colour of milk-ice. The mountainsides are strewn with amazing boulders and broken scraps made by ancient glaciers which once filled the whole valley of the Teberda. This is one of the most picturesque and wildest spots in the Caucasus. The mountains become immense; great scarps and

West of the Klukhor

slabs of black rock rise in jagged splendour to blot out the blue sky. You ride through dark forests of beech and oak, where waterfalls and foaming white streams pour and rush to join the Ganatchkir . . . and then a wandering ride, with heads bent, among the birch spinney; and you are out in an alpine valley.

A row of log cabins and a stone *kosh* lie among the rocks and glacial scrap of this valley. Sheep and goats browse on a few astonishing patches of green grass. In the old days, in the 1860's this was where a Tsarist barracks had been located. I saw no sign of them. But a poor-looking Karachaite crawled out of the *kosh*, and then dived back in it to come out and offer us the invariable bowl of sour milk. "No," he told us, "that is impossible! You will not get horses over the pass." Yusef replied: "We will see—if I have to carry these bags myself!"

In one stretch the valley became a gorge and we climbed, zigzagging up through rocks, away from a stream that fell almost a half-mile in a slanting waterfall. In places it foamed white as snow. The pine forests here were damp and dark as night. The rocks were completely covered with deep moss. Yusef pointed to a fifty-foot lump of rock—and to a peak overhead—saying that it had fallen from there last year. It had cut a path as wide as a city street through the forest—trees lying smashed like match-sticks. "When it rains heavily, the peaks crack—and the rocks come down," said Yusef. There was only one word for that scenery: staggering.

Freshfield says: ". . . immense walls of black rock with precipitous sides on which little snow lies. The summits, amongst which a Dru-like needle is remarkable, were unfortunately enveloped in fog, but they form a group of wild precipitous peaks, such as is seldom met with even in the Central Caucasus." This was when the great English alpine climber was back there in 1886, and on July 23rd tried to cross over the Nakar Pass to Utsch-Kalan, but was prevented by the obstinacy of the Teberdines, who said the path over the Nakar was impassable for beasts of burden, and who refused to act as porters. He had to return from the Klukhor Pass.

When we opened the main glacial valley a panorama of snow-clad grey peaks lay ahead of us. The snow was heavy on these, it being still June. A spectacle that made Yusef hunt about in the last hours of sunset to find two good stout staffs that he could cut into alpine stocks. "I think we will need these," he said grimly.

That night was spent in the crudest log cabin, if it could be called that, that I had slept in in the Caucasus. The space between the logs was in some places eight inches. In fact the cabin's dog tried to get in through one of them during the night, just over my head. There was no need for a hole in the roof for the smoke to leak out. Yet the old crone who was inhabiting it busied herself to make us comfortable. She showed us a necklace of old Tsarist coins that was apparently her greatest treasure. Then some buttons made from coins; about 75 kopecks in all. Some pathetic little silver seashells from a necklace which had once belonged to a child. And a rubber ball. Her man was away, she said; he was taking down a sick Russian (a G.P.U. man) to Teberda from the foot of the pass where he had been stationed. She also gave us some sour milk from the cattle we saw feeding in the flat valley.

I awoke in this shepherd's *kosh* about 6.30 and thought I would have a try for some lake trout. There was a little glacial tarn in the sump of the valley. I wanted to try a fly there as the sun rose over the high mountains and warmed the water. The Karachaites say that that is when the trout play—"You can see them jump!" I did. But they also saw me. The lake was so crystal clear that it was like looking down through thin air. I saw a few small and dark shapes shoot out into its centre. That was all. Then I did the next best thing. Stripped, and dived under into the icy water. The first seven seconds are the worst. . . . Then I hastily dried myself on my shirt and went back to the cabin for some tea and the cold eggs that Yusef and I had boiled before leaving Teberda, and we split the last tin of Marchand sardines, last of my iron rations. The woman in the hut was obviously frightened by the tinned fish when we offered her some, but she had made us some hot corn-pone on the embers of her fire. And with this sound breakfast in our stomachs we set out to cross the Klukhor Pass.

We struck off up the valley below that weird Dru-like needle, which I believe is one of the highest in the Caucasus, with constant waterfalls on our left. The path zigzagging up the mountain slopes soon struck into a forest of tall pine, through whose sighing points we occasionally caught glimpses of the bowl of snowy mountains we were climbing into. In this forest we found two Russians and a woman working on a freshly built log cabin. One of them was a G.P.U. guard, although he did not reveal it at that time. They were all cheery characters, and when we asked them was the snow hard enough to allow horses to be taken over the Klukhor all three immediately answered yes. From Yusef's lugubrious moan I could see that he did not believe them. Neither did I. And with this doubt in our minds we continued our climb. With the laughter of the Russians still in our ears we came out of the pine forest and into a world of prehistoric chaos. The great rock-chaos of the glacial age. Here we saw that the old zig-zig climb of the Military Road had been broken off the cliffs in places, or else for long sections were buried under heavy slides of snow. Here at about 7,000 feet we came up against heavy snowfields. Where they were in the shade of the grey peaks the surface was hard enough to bear the weight of a horse. Out in the sun, where the fields glistened with slush, our horses began to punch through. In their struggles they foundered themselves until they sank in, up to their bellies. The only thing to do was pull them over on their sides, flat as we could get them with their loads, then try to help them to their clever little feet again. Sometimes we made only a few yards. And the pack-horse, which was a weak little creature, soon tired; and we once or twice had to take her load off before we could get her upright again. This took most of the afternoon. The horses did not like where they were being taken; that was obvious. And we were tired. When we found a rock we usually sat down on it and had a good smoke. At the far end of one snowfield we found the body of a cow, which had been killed and half eaten by some animal. Yusef said that it had been done by a bear, that they frequently came over into this part of the Caucasus from the central forests. But snow had fallen since the cow had been killed, and we could find no tracks. Toward the end of the afternoon we reached the rocky trail going up the gorge of the pass. This was steep but clear from snow and the going was comparatively easy from then on. Our spirits rose.

Snow! We had climbed the last thousand feet or so to reach the glacial lake, and there it was — frozen. A few pools on its mottled surface were beginning to turn slushy green. Water poured through a broken gap in the snow shelf at its mouth and fell over the edge in a sheer drop of a thousand feet or so. Over this mouth, with a gap between them of only some twenty feet, projected two shelves of snow and ice. They looked strong enough to bear the weight of a man, and the water at the mouth was shallow enough to wade; but it was too tricky a spot to risk horses. We were stymied—400 feet below the Klukhor Pass.

XVI

IN my notes which I wrote as I perched on the edge of the glacial
lake that sunset I wrote the facetious comment: "I am silent on a
peak in the Caucasus . . . but if I am speechless, the mountains certainly are not!" It was one of the weirdest nights I have ever spent on
a mountain. Freshfield wrote that his Swiss guides did not like
climbing in the Caucasus, because on none of the ascents could they
get up and back the same day: they always had to spend at least one
night out, sleeping in the snow. Just as I was prepared to do now.
Only, they had known beforehand that they would have to do that,
and had the proper equipment. I sat there on a rock, with the actinic
rays boring into my skull (and it is amusing to note that a not-to-be-
outdone Soviet scientist of that time had just reported that actinic
rays penetrate the earth for two miles); wet from sweat and the slush
Yusef and I had mushed through getting our horses up to the lake,
and then trying to get them around it; wondering whether it would
be really worthwhile to spread out my bedroll on snow that was a
foot deep; while my ears buzzed with the sounds of falling water, and
every now and then I heard ominous rumbles and the report of
falling rocks. The mountains were "cracking" as they cooled. As
mountain climbing this was of course sheer child's play; and as for
exposure, it was no great hardship. Still—cold is cold; especially
when you cannot move about very much. And I had an area of
only a few feet of steep snow, the frozen lake, and then the drop of
the waterfall. I spent the night there.

I had sent Yusef back the minute we saw that we could not get
horses past the lake and I had unpacked the kit that I intended to
keep. I sent him back with two firm instructions: one was to tell the
Russians in the valley below just what we thought of them for telling
us that the pass was open for horses. The other was to get another
Karachaite, if he could find one, and bring him back to help carry
the kit over the worst of the Klukhor Pass. I sent the heavy duffle-

bag back with Yusef, leaving it to him to *cache* it and finally get it back to Wicksteed the best way he could. I watched him crossing the snowfields about a thousand feet below me; then I turned to the lake to see if we had missed any possible chance of circumventing it. It was beautiful, but indomitable. The pools on its melting surface were a bright emerald green. It was only five hundred yards wide at the most, narrowing at this end where an open stream of it poured in a thousand-foot drop into the lower valleys. It lay at the foot of a sheer wall of rock with, on my side, parts of the old Sukhuum Military Road still showing on it; and at its far end, blocking any conceivable progress, paused an ugly, grey-blue fan of glacier. Waterfalls, fine as spun silk, were falling from this sullen monster. And a small piece fell from it, thudding into the slush of the lake as I was looking at it. I sat there listening to the mountains cracking; and I no longer wondered why large sections of the old Sukhuum Military Road had broken off the cliffs.

The mountains rimmed this scene with a circle of jagged rocks and spurs. The towering Dru-like needle, opposite the waterfall, sticking up in the sky with not a foothold or slope of snow on it, turned blue and then black as the sun worked behind it. A white cloud began to form on its tip. As the sun sank it lighted up the emerald pools on the greyish lake, seemed to fire them with brilliant colour; then they too began to dull. Clouds began to lift up their heads behind the rim of mountains and pass along it. They were uncanny—their *movement*, in all this vast stillness. It was eerie, watching them—with the feeling that they were watching *me*. What are you going to do about it? they seemed to say. Then a misty shapelessness began to crawl down the dragon-like back of the glacier; it poured in and filled the bowl of the lake; every sound became muffled; and, opening my mouth, I breathed in the cold, damp air.

I had told Yusef, if he was lucky enough to find another Kara-chaite, for them both to bring up all the firewood they could carry, for this was far above the pass's timber-line. And I wanted my tea! Someone, at some time, had piled up a little square of rocks by the edge of the waterfall as a shelter against the winds which sweep through this pass. I kicked a place clear of snow inside this and managed to bring half a kettle of water to the boil, by using the whole of the last pack of solid-fuel tablets I had in my medical kit. Then

I found a board. Its discovery was miraculous: just the end of a split plank sticking out from where I had cleared the snow. It had lain too deep in snow to have become water-logged; and using some pages from my notebook I got some slivers I whittled from this to take fire. Then I made a whole pot of tea. Now I was happy; I had plenty of cigarettes, and I leaned back with some equanimity to watch night come on.

I spread out my bedroll and tried to use the slotted wood-case of my fishing-rod as a prop to hold up the groundsheet. It didn't work, but it did give enough cover for me to light a candle under it. I lay there writing notes of an experience I knew I was going to enjoy far much more after it was over. The most interesting thing was the way that all sounds seemed to die. The sounds of falling rock stopped entirely. The murmur of the waterfalls seemed to cease, except that from the big one by my side. The mist also began to vanish; stars appeared above the black ridges; and soon the mountain was freezing. So was I.

I was lying there thinking that I had got myself into about as inextricable a place as I could, if I wanted to change my mind about where I would spend the night; and, a little angrily, I thought of Yusef, curled up beside some fine fire down in the valley—when there he was! I heard a cry. And then two black heads appeared over the edge of snow; and Yusef and another Mohammedan climbed over. Yusef apologised for being away so long. I was recovering from my amazement that he had even thought of climbing back in the dark; they must have had the eyes of cats! They each unslung a large roll of dry sticks. We soon had some good strong heartening mugs of coffee. I had not recognised him, but Yusef said that this was the same man who had told us we would not get horses over the pass, when we had talked with him in the valley far below. Yusef had found him and his son tending some cows in the upper valley. This was encouraging, as we at least had a realist with us, not like those Russians! But the man was still gloomy about our chances of getting across even now. The sun was melting the snow, he said, and it was now soft and sliding. You couldn't *trust* it.

They took off their snow-moccasins and dried them on sticks before the fire. At the same time they warmed some dry hay which they had taken from their bags. Before they went to sleep they put these moccasins back on, stuffing their bare feet into the dry warm hay; then laced them up. They looked very comfortable. But I had no idea at all of how useful they could be—with the ganglion-knots of rawhide tied all around their foot-rim—until I saw them walk casually across steep snow-faces on which my brogues slipped, as if buttered, the next day. The knots sank in and took a good firm grip on the snow. They are very clever. These Karachaites, as the ancient Greeks reported, knew the use of the toboggan, and were using ice-irons and *crampons* long before the birth of Christ.

The amount of ground that Yusef must have covered was remarkable. Wicksteed speaks of Yusef's speed across mountains in his *Ten Years in Soviet Moscow:*

"... One day in his native village when he told me that he was going over the pass to the village that I had just come from with another guide, it occurred to me that it would be interesting to compare his rate of travelling with mine. I therefore asked him how long it would take him to get there. He looked at the sun and said, 'Well, if I start soon I shall be there before dark.' I may mention that it had taken Negley Farson and me a day and a half."

Wicksteed, who loved to Anglicise everything, always insisted on calling Yusef—Joseph; and the young man would reply, thinking that Wicker did not know how to pronounce his name correctly: "No! No, Dedushka"—he also called Wicksteed Grandpa—"Yuuu-zev! Yu-*sef*!" As to me, read what Wicksteed said of Yu-*sef*:

"Tarzan [a mysterious former companion of Wicksteed's long walks in the Caucasus] and Farson also won his high approval. The latter he always referred to as Negley Farson Chicago *Daily News* under the impression that his surname was News and that he had four Christian names."

We decided to start as soon as there was light enough to see by, before the sun could begin softening the snow. I had not the Caucasian's knack of just closing my eyes and falling to sleep as I did it. I may have dozed once or twice, but I sat there most of the night smoking, prudently putting another precious stick on the fire, having more coffee; and I was wide awake when the sky began to lighten. The dew had fallen on their black shaggy *burkas*; and there they lay, Yusef's head on the other man's legs, curled up like a couple of black bears. Morning came, a sky of mauve behind the high spear-tip, some light blue along the eastern cliffs, then a faint rose; but the lighting was pale and cold. The groundsheet fluttered in a sudden wind. . . . The sun was still a long way below the bend of the world yet. At 3 o'clock we could begin to distinguish the upper rocks; and a bear, or an ibex, started a slide above us. At 4 o'clock we put on all the firewood that was left, and made coffee.

We felt we were sitting on top of the world as we made that last meal. We split the kit, and I noticed that Yusef, with great presence of mind, gave the other Mohammedan the heavy bedroll to carry, in which I had wrapped up almost everything (see photo facing p. 128). Then with the sharpened long sticks that we had brought up last night we started to cross the lake. For me a fall off the snow shelf into the glacial lake was the prelude to the day. But we had to wade across the mouth of the lake anyway, to get to the far side; and I saved my camera from more than a quick dunking. It was an old—but *very* reliable—Eastman Kodak, postcard size, which, I believe, is not being made any more. But the first photo I took with it that morning shows clearly (see above photo facing p. 128): first, the grey glacial lake, in mid-foreground; the cliffs, with the various levels of the old Sukhuum Military Road zigzagging up them; a place, dead centre of photo, where the road had sheered off the cliff entirely; and, from the shadows cast by the Dru-like needle, as well as from ourselves, you can tell what time in the morning it was: about 6 o'clock. The debonair figure on the left is, of course—Yu-*sef!*

We were feeling rather good just at that moment. We climbed up the next shelf and around the sixty yards of snow-face that makes that trickiest part of the whole pass. There is a narrow footpath around this spur in August, when it is free from snow; here I slipped, and the stick heavily jammed in the snow, just saved me from going off it. There is a big drop. After we had got around that, step by cautious step, we thought there was nothing to it: just the long climb up the amazing big dome of snow which makes the very top of the Klukhor Pass. We, or at any rate I, felt that now the worst was over; and all that was left was the long trek on the other side until we found some shepherds and horses, perhaps a walk of two days.

But the other side held disillusionment. There was no trail. The snows went to the cliff edge and then dropped sheer into a valley that was as white as a bowl. In casting about to find some way to get around this impassable barrier of sliding snow we went down a little island of rocks that ran down its face and here we tested our luck. If we should slide off the snow and go down into the valley it might not be so bad. But if we slipped, and went over the ledge directly below us, it would be no good at all. We selected two boulders of about equal size and shape and sent them careering down the snow-face.

The first, gaining momentum every instant, thundered down the snow slope, splashed the snow like spray as it came down between flights, rolled the entire way across the valley at the bottom and part way up the opposite slope. Impressive—but comforting.

The next (see photo facing p. 129), taken from where we launched these two stones) started on precisely the same course, shot down from us and over the cliff—an experiment, which, as far as we were concerned settled the argument.

"It is better to live," said Yusef in a low voice.

Man proposes! . . . We did try to get out on the snow-face down which the first stone had curved; but after we had got only fifteen feet or so Yusef struck ice under the thin snow with his sharp stick, and waved us not to follow. One of the worst parts of the day, for me, was turning around on that snow-face—which I did by making footholds with my behind. I sat down to make the turn. Fifty yards and we might have done it. There is no use dwelling on the disgust and humiliation of having to turn back, the gloom that almost made me sick, and the feeling of doubt and uncertainty that plagued me when we got down, once more, to the snowfields below the pass. Better to live? I have often wondered since that day if Yusef was right; though we had no doubts on that sunny morning.

Crossing the snowfields going down we met a party of three men walking up to the pass. Two of them had gone over the previous year; and they smiled when my two Mohammedans told them about this year's snow—the worst one of them had seen in fifteen years. And he lived in this valley.

"Ho!—do you think that is going to stop *me*?" jeered their leader (Yusef told me afterward that he was the veteran guide of them all). "Why, I—I'll use *sticks*—I'll make a fence of sticks. Easy!"

Yusef looked almost white with gloom. "Ask the old man where he is going to get his sticks," I said to him. "Tell him he had better cut them now. He won't find any up there!"

*

Yusef brightened, but the old man just waved his big hand at him. "Go back," he said. "You don't know the pass." And they strode off. "Do you think he will do it?" I asked Yusef. "I don't know. It will be very bad for me if he does. . . . In my village, you know?"

I lay in the sun among the pine trees down below and drank the dregs of defeat. If those other men went over. . . . But they came back —trooping down the trail from the glacial-scrap just at dusk. They agreed with us now. "That's all right!" said the old man, when Yusef asked him why he had changed his mind. "I'm going over. I've come down here to make other arrangements."

What they were I shall never know. But two weeks later, when I was back in Moscow, I got a letter from old Wicksteed that made my heart sing with joy. It went something like this:

"Honour is satisfied. The old duffer came back again. He is here in the village now, making all kinds of excuses. A Sukhuum mountaineering doctor who came over the Klukhor in dead winter, when he said it was easy with the deep snow, is also back here in Teberda. So is a so-called alpine party of twenty-four Leningraders, who came down here to 'do' the Caucasus. . . . Joseph is in great form and sends you his best. . . . Cheer up; it was the trip of a lifetime, yours and mine; I will never forget it. . . ."

But that night when we came down from the pass, I lay beside the pine fire that Yusef had built seldom having felt lower in my life. Our horses, which had been hobbled, had lost themselves up another valley. They were not found until the next day. Then the long ride back. Back to Teberda and Wicksteed sitting by the window of our little board room which he, in splendid isolation, had already turned into a shambles.

"I knew you were coming," he said. "The 'mountain wireless' got word down last night that you could not get over. I expected you before this."

I slid down from my horse and told him how Yusef had been searching for our horses all the previous afternoon, and then I flung myself down on the cot, enduring the remarks of Yusef's fat father, who could hardly climb out of bed—the ice-irons he would have equipped himself with, steel-tipped alpine stocks, and so forth.

"Bless my soul!" smiled old Wicker, "what are you so surly about? Man proposes and God disposes—and don't you know that you just can't 'buy a railroad ticket' over the Caucasus?"

"Listen, Wicker," I exploded petulantly. "I am now going to arise, Alexander Wicksteed, go out and buy as many bottles of that strong Caucasian purple wine as I can get hold of—and get thoroughly plastered."

"Wait a minute!" he said, hastily putting on his sandals. "I'll go with you!"

*　　*　　*

We walked through the shimmering trees. "I have come to the conclusion," he said, as we were comfortably drinking in the local, "that the happiness—or the oblivion—that one gets from alcohol is not altogether illegitimate."

*　　*　　*

I rode for the next two days on a bone-breaking mountain cart to Batalpaschinsk, where I caught the train back to Moscow. In September, at my farewell party to my friends of the Press and some of the secretaries of the Diplomatic Corps, I made old Alexander Wicksteed the guest of honour. "Must I put on a tie?" he asked. "Lord no—just wear your stinking old Russian knee-boots, and, if you have one, a clean *rubashka*. You are to be the toastmaster."

His farewell speech was magnificent, and quite Wicksteedian.

"The more I have travelled the stupendous Caucasus with Farson," he began—he really looked splendid there at the head of the table: he had bought a cobalt-blue corduroy *rubashka* for the occasion, and, as he said, his beard covered the aperture where his necktie should have been—". . . the more I have trudged behind him up some of those breathless precipices, those Olympian peaks above which only the eagle soars, Farson, magnificent on his horse; the more I have seen him amid savage, unknown tribes . . ."

I sat there looking as modest as possible. The younger members of the Diplomatic Corps were gazing at me admiringly, my own newspaper colleagues looking, naturally, not quite so pleased.

Wicksteed went on: ". . . the more I picture him dealing with our porters, bargaining for our food, cooking our meals over those rose-red Caucasian campfires—and *what cooking*: I have never known

· 151 ·

anything like it!—the more do I begin to realise what a wonderful woman his wife must be."

*   *   *

That was the last I ever saw of him. Certainly the most congenial, witty, and unexpected man I have ever travelled with. To me, Wicksteed was the Caucasus. That is why this book is for him.

INDEX OF PLACE NAMES

CPSIA information can be obtained
at www.ICGtesting.com
Printed in the USA
LVHW081140060921
697094LV00004B/11